"Bill saw potential in me that I never saw in myself. From the very start, he instilled his thirty-plus years of real estate and business experience into me. He exists in a genius zone of being a family man first, a serial entrepreneur, and the GOAT of real estate investing. Without Bill, I wouldn't be able to inspire and help thousands of investors. Read this book twice, then read it again."

—Ryan Bakke, CPA, real estate investor, and entrepreneur

"Starting with the ambition to leave my W2 and a goal to achieve financial freedom, I joined Bill's mastermind program. Through his guidance, I modeled his expertise in STR investing and management, marketing, and revenue optimization and built two successful companies in just two years. Bill's coaching has led me to greater financial success, more time freedom, and a significantly improved quality of life. I am deeply grateful for his role in transforming my life and the future of my family."

—Emile Sakhel, real estate investor and founder of Pricing By Mira

Super Properties: Your Step-by-Step Guide to Making $250,000 Per Year from Airbnbs with One Up-Front Investment

For more information, please contact:
Amplify Publishing, an imprint of Amplify Publishing Group
620 Herndon Parkway, Suite 220
Herndon, VA 20170
info@amplifypublishing.com

Library of Congress Control Number: 2025910355

CPSIA Code: PRV0725A

ISBN-13: 979-8-89138-709-6

Printed in the United States

PRAISE FOR
SUPER PROPERTIES

"There are educators, there are coaches, and then there are visionaries—men who don't just teach an industry but transform it. Bill Faeth is one of those rare forces of change. In the world of Airbnb investing, where fortunes are made and lost, Bill stands as a guiding light. His wisdom, experience, and relentless passion don't just help people make money—they unlock generational wealth. If financial freedom through real estate is your goal, then look no further. This book and Bill's teachings aren't just lessons; they are a roadmap to a future most only dream of. Few walk this earth with the integrity, insight, and impact of Bill Faeth. A legendary entrepreneur, an extraordinary father, a devoted husband, and a friend whose influence will echo for years to come."

—Pace Morby, TV host, author, investor, entrepreneur, speaker, and the GOAT of creative financing

"Bill has the rare talent of being both a brilliant real estate investor and one of the best educators in the industry. This book not only defies conventional wisdom; it gives a proven roadmap to break free from the rat race and build lasting wealth. Don't read this book unless you're serious about creating the life of your dreams!"

—**Jerry Norton,** founder, Flipping Mastery

"Bill Faeth has been an invaluable mentor in my short-term rental journey. His ability to simplify complex strategies and provide a clear, no-nonsense approach has made a huge impact on my business. Thanks to his guidance, I've been able to grow with confidence and avoid costly mistakes. Bill genuinely cares about helping others succeed, and his expertise in marketing and operations is second to none. If you're serious about success in short-term rentals, learning from Bill is one of the best investments you can make."

—**Kenny Bedwell,** founder of STR Insights, real estate investor, and entrepreneur

To my wife, Brea,
and our two amazing daughters,
Gentry and Oaklee.

$UPER PROPERTIES

PROPERTIES

Your Step-by-Step Guide
to Making $250,000 Per Year
from Airbnbs with
One Up-Front Investment

BILL FAETH

BUILD
SHORT TERM RENTAL
WEALTH

CONTENTS

Resources x

Foreword 1

Introduction: Early Lessons 3

1. Mastering the Short Game 13

2. Getting Ready 29

3. The Four Pillars of Investing 43

4. The 250 Plan 61

5. Starting with No Money 71

6. Choosing Your Market 79

7. Property Selection and Underwriting 93

8. Offer to Close and Install (Plus a Secret Bonus) 105

9. Setting Up Your Listing and Marketing ... 113

10. Technology and Automation 131

11. Pricing Optimization 141

Conclusion: The Entire Country Is Your Oyster 147

Acknowledgments 153

About the Author 155

RESOURCES

Whether you're brand new or scaling fast, these resources are designed to help you make smarter, faster decisions—and avoid costly mistakes. These are the exact tools I personally use and recommend. Since I reference them periodically throughout the book, some familiarity with them would be helpful.

Super Property Grader: Not all properties are created equal. The Super Property Grading System helps you assess a property's potential with precision so you can spot high-performing investments and know *exactly* which ones are worth your time.

buildstrwealth.com/superpropertygrader

Proforma: Analyze whether a deal is worth your time or a hard pass with this tool that clearly breaks down what income and expenses to expect and provides forecasts of how the deal aligns with your investment goals. This is the same tool Jon "The Bank Whisperer" Hodge and I use to underwrite deals.

At the link below, you'll find a video that walks you step-by-step through how we use it.

buildstrwealth.com/proforma

DTI Calculator: Instead of letting banks dictate your future, use this calculator to figure out exactly what you can borrow before you apply.

buildstrwealth.com/dticalculator

Want even more? We've put the best of the best all in one place. Head to our Resources Hub at buildstrwealth.com/resources to access our most powerful tools, trainings, and communities we recommend—or just scan the QR code below to get there fast.

FOREWORD

Kenny Bedwell,

founder, STR Insights

When I first came across Bill Faeth, I had no idea how much of an impact he would have on my journey. His insights into short-term rentals and business strategy weren't just theories—they were proven, actionable steps that transformed the way I approached my work.

Bill has a unique ability to break down complex strategies into simple, practical steps. Through his mentorship, I gained the confidence and tools to grow, pivot, and scale in ways I hadn't thought possible. His guidance not only helped me build a more profitable business but also reinforced the importance of integrity, generosity, and serving others in the industry.

More than just a coach, Bill is a leader who genuinely cares about the success of those he mentors. His teachings have shaped the way I approach short-term rentals, marketing, and leadership, and I am incredibly grateful for the impact he has had on my business and life.

For anyone looking to learn from one of the best in the industry, this is it. Bill Faeth's wisdom, experience, and generosity will change the way you think about business—and more importantly, how you take action.

INTRODUCTION

EARLY LESSONS

When I was a kid growing up in Bakersfield, California, *wealth* wasn't even in my vocabulary. My single mother, a teacher, never made more than $30,000 a year in the late 1970s and early 1980s. Sure, we didn't miss meals. But vacations and luxury? Those weren't part of our world.

That is, until I got my first taste of something special.

When I was eight or nine, I visited Pismo Coast Village in Pismo Beach with a friend. It was my first time seeing the ocean. The drive from Bakersfield took us through dead, brown hills. Not much to look at. But man, when we hit that beach, it was incredible.

That first beach trip, we stayed in a twenty-year-old trailer. Not even an RV, just a fifth wheel. Old, dingy, run-down. But for us? It was paradise. My mother couldn't join us, as she was back home teaching summer school, working two jobs to keep us afloat.

Now at age fifty, I realize that experience planted the seed for something bigger than a dream—it became my driving force. That kid who couldn't afford a proper beach vacation now owns multiple short-term rentals, including the first-ever beach house I bought with my wife, Brea. For me, that purchase was not just about having a vacation home—it was about transforming that childhood memory of a rusty fifth wheel into creating amazing experiences for other families.

In doing so, I've built generational wealth that my eight-year-old self couldn't even imagine. This isn't just comfortable living. I'm talking about having more than enough to take care of my kids' futures, support my in-laws, give my wife the security she deserves, and make sure our whole family is protected.

That generational scarcity that I grew up with? It stopped with me.

And now? My mission is to help you do the same thing. Building wealth through short-term rentals isn't just about making money—it's about breaking through whatever limitations you grew up with and creating a legacy that impacts generations.

I have developed a system that works, and I'm here to show you exactly how to do it.

LEARNING THE FUNDAMENTALS

Everything changed when I was fifteen. My mother, after decades of saving, made her first real investment. Until then, she'd only owned two houses: one during her marriage to my father (they divorced when I was five), and our current home in south Bakersfield—a modest three-bedroom, two-bath house from the mid-1970s.

That year, she saw an opportunity that aligned perfectly with her life's work: buying and running a preschool called Happy Land Learning Center. It was a small operation—just two buildings on barely an acre of land. She gave me my first job there, raking leaves and cleaning the yard on weekends. I'll be honest . . . I hated every minute of it. But through those long weekends of yard work, my mother was teaching me something invaluable: hard work. Whenever I asked her how to get ahead in life, that was always her answer.

My friend Pace Morby shares a similar story in his book, *Wealth without Cash*, about how his father would constantly reinforce that same message: "It just takes hard work." That was my mother's mantra, too. She didn't have entrepreneurial skills or business experience, but the lessons she instilled in me at that young age would later shape how I approached launching thirty-seven different startups.

For a year and a half, I watched my mother struggle with the business's finances. Every night, our dining room table disappeared under a maze of papers, and even though my mother had been keeping handwritten ledgers, neither of us really understood what profit and loss meant.

That all changed the day an older gentleman came over and sat at that table. He took one look at all those scattered papers and gave us both our first real business lesson. He explained, "You take all of your expenses," as he put them onto one side of the ledger. "Then here's all your income, your revenue—what the parents are paying for their children, the late fees—all of that goes on the right side. Now, let's add up these expenses and subtract them from your income: taxes, mortgage payments, property costs, payroll, everything."

Profit and Loss

Revenue	Expenses
• _____	• _____
• _____	• _____
• _____	• _____
• _____	• _____
• _____	• _____
• _____	• _____
• _____	• _____

Profit: $_____

It seems so simple now. But for us at the time? It was revolutionary. For the first time, about a year and a half into running the business, my mother finally understood exactly where she stood financially.

That moment taught me that success isn't just about working hard. It's about understanding your numbers—*really* understanding them. Today, when I create tools for short-term rental investors like my Proforma and the Super Property Grader, I think back to that dining room table and the confidence that came once there was finally clarity on the preschool's finances. Every property, every investment, every business decision comes down to those same basic principles my mother and I learned that day.

These early lessons are the foundation of everything I teach about building wealth through short-term rentals. Success isn't just about buying properties—it's about applying these fundamental truths in a way that creates value for others while building wealth for yourself.

MY FIRST BUSINESS VENTURE

That simple lesson at our dining room table would soon come full circle with my first real business venture.

It started at a junior pro-am golf tournament in Southern California, where I met Jay Jacoby, owner of American Pacific T-Shirt Company. We spent four and a half hours playing golf but actually talking about basketball. I was a die-hard Lakers fan—Magic Johnson was my hero, along with Kareem Abdul-Jabbar, James Worthy, Byron Scott, Kurt Rambis, and the whole squad. Though I'd never been able to afford seeing them in person, I never missed a game on the local TV station KTLA.

After our round, Jacoby walked us to the parking lot and opened his trunk. Inside were five T-shirts—none of them Lakers gear. There was Karl Malone from the Utah Jazz, Charles Barkley with the Houston Rockets, Larry Bird (whom I despised, as he was Magic's nemesis), and Michael Jordan from the Chicago Bulls. Even though Jordan was the best in the NBA, I didn't even want *his* shirt. Still, I thanked Mr. Jacoby and took them home.

About a week later, Mom asked, "Hey, where are all those T-shirts? Those really cool shirts that Mr. Jacoby gave to you?" I ignored her, hoping she wouldn't ask again.

"Billy, where are those shirts?" she asked again minutes later.

Finally, I had to look her in the eye. "Mom, I sold them."

"You did *what*?"

"I sold them for $25 each."

"You sold those shirts Mr. Jacoby gave you as a *gift*?" Then she motioned for me to sit down.

"I need you to give me that money," she explained. "And the next time we see Mr. Jacoby, we're giving it back."

Sure enough, a few months later, at another tournament in Pasadena, we ran into him. My mother had been carrying that envelope of money to every tournament, waiting for this moment. I was terrified, but I approached him anyway.

"Mr. Jacoby, I sold the shirts." To my surprise, he smiled.

"That's okay. Why don't you guys come to my house? I'll buy you lunch."

When my mother explained we needed to get back to Bakersfield, his eyes lit up.

"You know what, Billy? I don't even sell these shirts for $25," he said, as though he was thinking out loud. "If you want to sell shirts, I'll give you a couple boxes—about a hundred T-shirts—to take back to Bakersfield. I'll give your mom my address and number, and we'll split the profits fifty-fifty."

That night, I could barely contain my excitement. "Mom, can I put one of these boxes in the back seat?" I tore into them immediately. First, I pulled out all the Lakers shirts—a Kareem Abdul-Jabbar, two Magic Johnsons, and one James Worthy. "Mom, I want to keep these."

"You have to pay for them," she said firmly. We'd agreed to pay Mr. Jacoby $5 per shirt and split anything above that.

That night, back at our dining table, Mom helped me create my first profit and loss statement over a plate of Hamburger Helper and a rare treat of Coca-Cola. We calculated everything: gas ($18), future In-N-Out Burger stops ($15), and the cost of the shirts. Seventy shirts at $20 each meant $1,400 in revenue, split in half. That $700 potential profit was my first real lesson in understanding the difference between revenue and net income.

$$\boxed{\$20 \times 70} \quad \boxed{\$18 + \$15 + \$5 \times 70}$$
$$\textbf{Shirt Sales - Expenses / 2 = Profit}$$
$$\$1{,}400 - \$383 / 2 = \boxed{\$508.50}$$

LET'S GET STARTED

That early lesson in understanding numbers is why I created a complete system for short-term rental success. At its core is the 250 Plan—a strategy to build a small but mighty portfolio of Super Properties that consistently generate $250,000 or more in net annual income. But to execute this plan, you need the right tools to make smart decisions.

It starts with my DTI (debt-to-income) calculator, which helps you understand your bankability and what you can actually afford. Then there's the Super Property Grader, which takes the guesswork out of when to pull the trigger on a property. Finally, my detailed Proforma tool guides you through the underwriting process, ensuring that you catch every expense—something I learned the hard way in Banner Elk, North Carolina, when I missed a $4,000 snow-plowing expense in my calculations. See the Resources section at the beginning of this book for ways to download these tools.

When you combine these tools, you have everything you need to identify Super Properties—the kind that don't just generate income but *build lasting wealth*. This book will show you exactly how to create and optimize these properties step-by-step, from identifying the right markets to implementing systems that maximize your revenue.

And here's the best part: you don't need money to get started. You can start with zero dollars. I'm not talking about rental arbitrage, either. I'm talking about safe, sound investments that generate cash flow, grow in appreciation, and give you the ability to reposition and scale—even if you're starting with no capital.

Finally, I want to address something early on so we can clear the air around it. I know some people think short-term rentals are risky today, post-COVID. They're not risky—the market is just maturing. There are more players, higher prices, and greater challenges to finding good deals. The lazy investors have dropped out, or they settled for poor investments during COVID.

I'm going to shoot you straight. No bullshit. No sales pitch. Just an unfiltered approach to investing in real estate and making $250,000 in net income from one up-front investment.

CHAPTER 1

MASTERING THE SHORT GAME

Most real estate investors fail before they even start. Why? Because they buy the wrong property in the wrong market with the wrong plan—and they don't even realize it until it's too late.

Now, before you think I'm just another investor jumping on the short-term rental trend, let me be clear: my real estate journey started thirty-one years ago, and it began in an unlikely place—professional golf.

In 1991, I was the third-ranked golfer in the world coming out of high school, with full-ride scholarship offers from over forty Division One universities. I chose UCLA, but after four months, I knew it wasn't for me. At nineteen, I dropped out to turn pro—a decision that didn't sit well with my family of educators. My mother, grandfather, and grandmother were all teachers, and they saw me throwing away a full scholarship they could never have afforded. They cut off their support, leaving me to make it on my own.

That first year on the pro circuit, I managed to make enough money to catch the attention of my CPA, Jeff. Instead of letting me blow it in Vegas or on travel, he guided me toward my first investment: a $198,000 duplex in Bakersfield, California. That was my introduction to real estate, and from there, the journey only grew.

Over the next three decades, I explored every corner of real estate. I built the first industrial Gold LEED-certified commercial building in Nashville for my ground transportation company. I invested in single-family homes, long-term rentals, multifamily properties, and even boutique motels. But it wasn't until 2015 that I discovered short-term rentals—and that discovery happened by accident.

THE GULF SHORES GAME-CHANGER

Since 2015, I've focused primarily on short-term rentals for one simple reason: the cash flow is three to five times greater than long-term rentals. Back then, a $450,000 condo in downtown Nashville might get you $2,000 a month in long-term rental income. As a short-term rental? Seven to nine thousand dollars a month.

My venture (along with my wife, Brea) into short-term rentals started over lunch with old friends, William and Mary Beth Wilson, who own one of the largest property management companies in Destin, Florida. William and I go way back—we played professional golf together on the South American PGA Tour.

I laid it out straight for him: "Hey, I've got about $126,000, and we'd love to buy a place here. But Brea has some contingencies . . . She wants to be able to hear the waves, see the ocean, and smell the salt air."

William just laughed. "You're not going to be able to get something like that here." This was 2015, pre-COVID, when prices were different. "What you guys need to do," he said, "is check out this place called Gulf Shores."

Known as the "Redneck Riviera" for Nashville and Atlanta folks, Gulf Shores turned out to be exactly what we needed. We looked at ten properties, but as you've probably already guessed, we ended up buying the very first one that caught our eye.

Like most beginners, we thought using a property manager was the safe play for our first short-term rental. We were wrong.

THE PROPERTY MANAGER MISTAKE

Now, you might be thinking, "Bill, why would someone who teaches short-term rental wealth use a property manager?"

We were complete newbies to short-term rentals and had yet to learn that they're a whole different game from long-term rentals or multifamily properties. The property manager projected $45,000 in annual revenue, which sounded good to us. But we learned real quick that they didn't give a shit about our success.

After ninety days of mediocre service, we had to make a tough call. You see, this wasn't just another investment for us. We were still recovering from the Nashville flood in 2010 and the recession. That $126,000 investment was everything we had—we couldn't afford to make a mistake. We couldn't afford to stay with a property manager who wasn't delivering.

So we fired them and took over everything ourselves. No experience, just determination. We handled it all: pricing optimization on Airbnb and Vrbo, guest communication, cleaning crew, handyman—the whole nine yards. This desperation, this need to make it work, became the foundation of what would become the 250 Plan.

To turn it around, we immediately implemented three key changes:

1. **Dynamic Pricing:** Ditched their outdated fixed seasonal rates and started adjusting prices weekly based on demand.

2. **Guest Experience Upgrades:** Overhauled the listing photos, improved amenities, and focused on getting better reviews.

3. **Proactive Marketing:** Stopped relying solely on Airbnb and started building relationships with past guests.

The results? We hit $98,000 in revenue that first year—and that's including those three shitty months under the property manager. The next year? $112,000. If we'd stuck with the property manager, we would've been losing money instead of building wealth.

Pro Tip: Our property in Gulf Shores was located in Tier Two at the beach—not beachfront, but one row back. You could still see the ocean, hear the waves, and smell the salt air. Tier Two often gives you the best returns in beach markets. I'll dive deeper into this strategy in the Property Selection chapter.

This experience was our *real* start in short-term rentals. It's where we cut our teeth and learned fast. *Real fast.* That increased cash flow didn't just validate our decision—it funded our second short-term rental and launched us toward building real wealth.

THE 250 PLAN: YOUR PATH TO $250,000

Before we dive deep into the details, let me share the destination: the 250 Plan. It's simple but powerful. Let me be clear though—it's not a get-rich-quick scheme.

Here's what it looks like:

- Starting point: One up-front investment
- Goal: Grow your portfolio to five properties
- Timeline: Five years
- Result: $250,000 in net income annually ($50,000 per property)

The 250 Plan

The 250 Plan

+ $50,000
+ $50,000
+ $50,000
+ $50,000
+ $50,000

We start small and level up with each purchase. Every property decision—whether buying, managing, selling, or repositioning—focuses on four critical components:

1. Cash Flow
2. Appreciation
3. Debt Paydown
4. Tax Benefits

The 4 Pillars of
Real Estate Investing

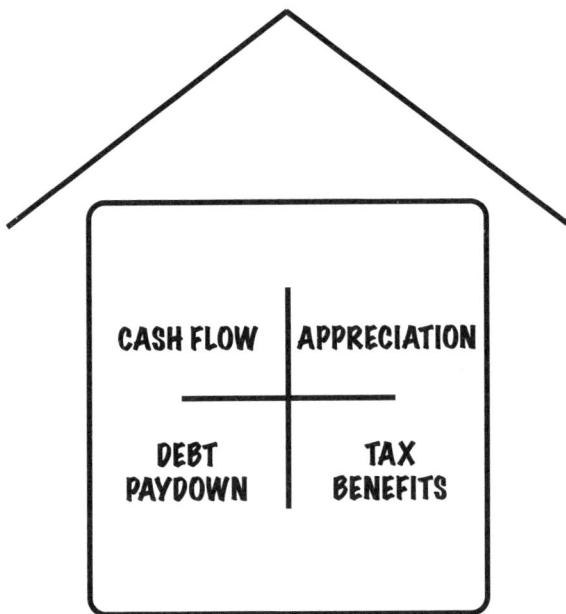

| CASH FLOW | APPRECIATION |
| DEBT PAYDOWN | TAX BENEFITS |

When you master these four components and understand how to evaluate and optimize each one, you'll be ready to execute the 250 Plan. Plus, when you add in strategies like repositioning, creative financing, and accelerating debt paydown (which we'll cover in detail later) and lock in seller concessions, you can accelerate your progress dramatically. It's like throwing gas on a fire.

Now, you might be wondering . . . how do we actually achieve these numbers?

That's where Super Properties come in.

WHAT IS A SUPER PROPERTY?

A Super Property is the vehicle that makes the 250 Plan work. It's not about having the biggest properties or the largest portfolio. It's about consistently outperforming the entire marketplace in both revenue and return on investment. My wife and I have proven this model works across every price point:

- A one-bedroom condo we bought for $559,000
- A $3,000,000 estate in Whitefish, Montana, with two houses, a pond, and a river on five-and-a-quarter acres
- And everything in between

We've lived in Nashville for twenty-three years, but we've never made a short-term rental investment there. Our properties span from Montana to Arizona, from North Carolina to

Alabama. We focus on secondary markets—Gulf Shores instead of 30A, Banner Elk instead of the Smokies, Cave Creek instead of Scottsdale, Whitefish instead of Big Sky.

We leverage every ounce of knowledge and effort into making these properties exceptional. Why? Because in today's maturing market, average properties get average results—and average isn't good enough for the 250 Plan.

Remember: This isn't about creating just another rental property. It's about building an elevated experience that consistently outperforms the market. That's what makes a Super Property super . . . and that's what makes the 250 Plan achievable.

But before we dive into creating these exceptional properties, let's talk about risk management. There are some critical things you need to know about risks, wrong assumptions, and where *not* to invest.

THE TWO BIGGEST RISKS IN SHORT-TERM RENTALS

There are a lot of myths and misconceptions about investing in short-term rentals that I'm going to break down for you. Before we really dive in, however, let's address the two biggest risks in our industry and how to mitigate them.

Risk #1: Regulation

Regulation is one of our biggest challenges, primarily because of the affordable housing debate. In some markets, short-term rentals *do* affect affordable housing; in others, however, they don't. Regardless, it can absolutely be a serious concern for communities and their workforce. Think about it—we need servers, bellmen, and janitors. These are necessary jobs in our country, but they're not usually high-paying positions.

The impact on affordable housing hits hardest in urban areas. That's exactly why I don't own a single property in an urban market. Well . . . technically, as of this writing, I am under contract for a property in downtown New Orleans, two blocks from Bourbon Street. But it's not a short-term rental—it's a motel I'm buying with my friend Kenny Bedwell from STR Insights.

Kenny's not just any partner—he's the absolute best property finder in this industry and an OG in my mastermind. Over the five years we've known each other, I've watched him develop STR Insights into one of the best data analytics tools for underwriting properties. When someone like Kenny, with his deep market knowledge, chooses to invest in urban areas only through motels and hotels, that should tell you something.

That said, I wouldn't touch a single-family home or condo in downtown New Orleans or any urban market. That's where regulation rears its ugly head the most, and it's where the affordable housing debate has the strongest impact.

Risk #2: Lack of Consistency

The second major threat to our industry is inconsistency in guest experience. As someone who travels constantly for business—speaking engagements, boot camps in eleven states last year alone, etc.—I've seen this firsthand. I'm a Marriott guy. Why? Because of consistency. When you book a Marriott or Hilton, you know exactly what you're getting: the bed type, the linens, even the room layout. It helps you plan and helps you pack.

But short-term rentals? You never know what you're going to get, whether you book through Airbnb, Vrbo, or Expedia. Even large portfolio holders with fifty or one hundred properties can't maintain consistency. And from host to host? The experience can change dramatically.

As Forrest Gump said, "Life is like a box of chocolates . . ." But you don't want your renter experience to be.

This inconsistency is more than just an annoyance. It's a fundamental problem in our industry. When guests have a negative experience, it doesn't just affect that one property or that one host. It erodes trust in the entire short-term rental market. These disappointed travelers start looking at hotels again, where at least they know what they're getting.

THE CUSTOMER LOYALTY PROBLEM

Another concern I've seen, particularly if someone is not new to owning a business but they are new to the short-term rental industry, is the (at best) marginal customer loyalty.

Think about your favorite restaurant. One bad experience? You'll probably give it another shot if they handle it right. A second mediocre meal? Now you're asking, "Should we try somewhere else?"

The problem with short-term rentals is that we don't have that built-up loyalty. People simply aren't booking the same property year after year, like they did twenty years ago.

Sure, you've got those families who've been going to the Outer Banks for decades, staying in the same tired property because of nostalgia. But for first-time guests? They walk in, smell must, sit on a dusty couch, find bent silverware and Brady Bunch wallpaper . . . they're not coming back unless they absolutely have to.

Legacy property managers are notorious for what I call the "property manager starter kit." Picture this: you book a five-bedroom house for twelve or fourteen people—maybe two families or a group of friends. You arrive to find one roll of paper towels, one roll of toilet paper, and one towel per person for a five-night stay. Suddenly, you're doing dishes and laundry every single day of your vacation. Talk about miserable.

Even within the same management company, the experience can vary wildly from property to property. You might have a terrible stay at one house and a five-star experience at another.

That's why I'm obsessive about being a consistent host. While we don't use identical furniture across all our properties, we maintain strict standards for essentials. Every bathroom gets the same high-quality toilet paper and towels—two per guest, with extras in the hallway closet. Every bathroom starts with three to five rolls of toilet paper. Every kitchen has four to five rolls of paper towels and enough place settings for everyone—three sets of silverware per guest, plenty of plates, cups, and wine glasses. We stock our properties the way we'd want our own homes stocked.

* * *

There is still a lot of preliminary work to do before we get into the weeds (and we will—just keep reading). But for now, it's enough to have mastered these key elements—and remain flexible enough to adjust as you go—for launching a successful short-term rental venture.

None of this matters, however, if you don't know *why* you're doing it.

CHAPTER 2

GETTING READY

Before you start browsing Zillow or scouting different markets, let's talk about getting ready—mentally and strategically.

There's a sequence to smart decision-making, and it starts with one fundamental question: *Why are you making this purchase?*

UNDERSTANDING YOUR *WHY*

In my experience, most people fall into one of two primary buckets when investing in real estate:

- Bucket #1: Lifestyle Assets
- Bucket #2: Pure Investments

Bucket 1: Lifestyle Assets

These are the dream properties—the beach house, the lake retreat, the cozy cabin near your favorite ski town, or that Orlando home to crash at after Disney. You're buying with personal use in mind. The property still needs to make money, but there's emotion involved. You're imagining family holidays, summer memories, or frequent getaways.

Bucket 2: Pure Investments

These are properties purchased solely for return. There's no emotional attachment, and you don't plan to stay there. You're focused on cash flow, appreciation, tax benefits, and repositioning opportunities. It's a business move from day one.

Let's start with **Bucket 1**, because this is where many new investors begin—and where most people make costly mistakes if they're not aligned.

You see a property that checks all the boxes. It's got charm, it's in a place you love, and you start picturing your family there. But you haven't run the numbers. You haven't had the hard conversations with your spouse. You haven't checked regulations or even confirmed it will create cash flow. Now you're emotionally attached, and it's hard to walk away—even if it's a bad deal.

That's why alignment is Step One.

If you're married or in a partnership, sit down and talk it out:

- Why are we buying this?
- Is it really for investment—or is it for lifestyle?
- Are we comfortable using this asset personally *and* financially?

These conversations aren't just about money. They protect your relationship, eliminate surprises, and set you up for success. My wife, Brea, and I have been doing this since 2015. Every week, we sit down and review our investments, our criteria, and our goals. We don't move forward unless we're 100 percent aligned on price, cash needed, timeline, and vision.

Now let's talk about **Bucket 2**, the pure investors.

This group is clear-eyed from day one. They're not emotionally tied to using the property themselves. Every decision is based on numbers:

- What's my cash-on-cash return?
- What's the gross vs. net revenue?
- How long is my payback period?
- What's the equity potential and exit strategy?

You might never step foot in the property—and that's fine. You're optimizing for profit, not personal use. That means you're using tools like AirDNA, STR Insights, and my Super Property Grader (see the Resources page at the beginning of this book for more information). You're digging into pro formas, traffic drivers, market data, and price comps. And you're not just hoping it performs—you're engineering it to do so.

There is no wrong bucket. You can do incredibly well in either *as long as you're clear on which one you're in.* The biggest mistakes happen when people try to straddle the line without clarity.

So, before we talk about market research or property selection, ask yourself honestly:

Am I buying for lifestyle, or am I buying for return?

Because every strategy from this point forward should flow from that answer.

SETTING A BUDGET

Let's talk budget.

Before you say, "Well, Bill, budget's a given," have you considered your budget *beyond* the price of the property and what your monthly payment will be?

In fact, if you are not in a position to pay cash outright, do you know how much down payment you can afford? Can you afford *any* sort of down payment? Don't worry, we are going to address each of these scenarios.

How much cash do you have to invest in a piece of real estate today, and what's your total purchase price? If you have $200,000 in cash, you don't have enough cash to buy a million-dollar property. Even though it takes 20 percent down, you still have closing costs, and there's no such thing as a turnkey property.

Let me repeat: *there's no such thing as a turnkey property*.

With $200,000 in cash, you're realistically looking at a maximum purchase price around $700,000. Why? Because that $700,000 property will need about $150,000–$160,000 for down payment and closing costs, leaving you $40,000–$50,000 for furnishings, decorations, and renovations. Honestly, $600,000–$650,000 is an even better target. Get these numbers nailed down before you do anything else.

For a $700,000 Property

$$\$200,000 = \$150,000 + \$50,000$$

| Cash | Down Payment | Furniture & Renovations |

Part of budgeting also includes determining your bankability. They are not the same.

Simply put, *bankability* will assist in figuring out your budget. Depending on your financial situation, it can also throw water on it. Stay with me here, because even though bankability gives you a hard dose of reality, it also gives you direction on which path to take in order to move forward and ultimately purchase a property.

Bankability involves knowing your debt-to-income (DTI) ratio, especially if you're going for a second home loan via Fannie Mae and Freddie Mac. Even for commercial loans, they'll want a personal financial statement. You can access a great DTI calculator created by Brenna Carles at The Mortgage Shop, plus training on what data to plug in, by following the link on the Resources page at the beginning of this book.

Your budget may also be seriously impacted by your marital status.

If You're Married

When filing taxes jointly as a couple, both spouses get access to the income on that tax return. But debt works differently—it's individual. You can use this to your advantage in real estate investing when using commercial loans.

For example, if you and your spouse are making $500,000 a year, it doesn't matter if it's $500,000 and zero or $250,000 and $250,000 split between spouses—you both get to utilize that full $500,000 in income to qualify for your next purchase. The debt side, though? That's where it gets interesting. If both your names are on your primary residence mortgage, let's say $2,000 a month, that affects both of your debt-to-income ratios. When buying investment properties, only one spouse needs to be the buyer, while the other can carry any consumer debt, like vehicles, credit cards, or student loans.

In my family, my wife carries all the "bad" debt. In our case, most of our bad debt is vehicles—Brea's Tesla, my daughter's vehicle, and my Ford F-150. I don't own any of that. I am the person who buys real estate, which I consider "good" debt.

Now, we typically put about 30 to 40 percent down, so the debt is not that heavy, nor does it show up on my credit report because I do not sign for it. That splitting of debt—having one spouse be the debtor and one spouse be the real estate investor with no bad debt—is going to help improve credit scores. It's going to help improve your personal financial statement. It's going to give you more buying power. But it needs to be done well in advance.

If You're Single

If you're single, managing your debt-to-income becomes even more critical because you can't split income and debt like married couples can.

Here are some tips if you're investing solo:

- Treat your credit card like a debit card. Use it for purchases but pay it off weekly. Carrying a balance can crush your DTI ratio and credit score.
- Know your credit reporting date. Every card reports to credit bureaus on a specific day (often the 12th to 14th of the month). Make sure your card balances are paid down before that date—not just by your statement due date—so the bureaus see a low balance.
- Ask for credit limit increases. About every six months, call your card issuer and request a limit increase without a hard pull. Expanding your available credit improves your utilization ratio, which boosts your score. Even a $2,000–$5,000 increase boosts your available credit, improving your DTI ratio.
- Open one new credit card each year and never close old ones. Even if you never use it, keeping it open builds your credit history. You might take a tiny credit

dip short-term, but the long-term gain from added credit history and higher limits far outweighs the risk.

- Keep utilization under 10 percent overall and under 3 percent per card if possible. The lower, the better when you're preparing for financing.

Your credit score will determine your financing options. In today's lending environment, rates are tiered by score ranges:

- 750+ = best rates
- 725 to 750 = slightly higher
- 700 to 725 = higher still
- Below 700 = significant rate increases

For example, a 750+ credit score might qualify you for 7 percent, while a 675 score might bump you to 8.25 percent.

That difference can cost tens of thousands over the life of a loan.

You can monitor your credit progress with free tools like Credit Karma or by pulling reports directly from TransUnion, Equifax, or Experian.

Don't wait until you're ready to buy to start fixing your credit—start now.

Improving your bankability isn't just about qualifying. It's about getting better terms, saving money, and building long-term wealth faster.

SELECTING A MARKET

Whether you have zero budget or $400,000 in cash, you also need to determine where you'll get more bang for your buck. It's an old cliché, but it's true: location, location, location. Once your budget is set, you'll want to consider the markets. A $200,000 budget will go far in some places and not so far in others.

Here's something I believe strongly, however: you need to have a genuine interest in any market you invest in. Even if you're making a purely financial decision with zero emotion involved, you still need to care about the area. Let me share a story that illustrates this.

My good friend Jon Hodge—I call him the Bank Whisperer—has made serious money in Hot Springs, Arkansas. He's been in my mastermind for three years and is on my super team. There's nothing wrong with Hot Springs, but when I visited to look at a property, it just didn't click for me. We had a partnership ready to go, but I passed because I couldn't get excited about the market. And here's the truth: if you're not excited about a market, you won't give it 100 percent, and that's a very expensive price to pay.

Moral of the story: don't invest your money if you cannot invest your enthusiasm, whether that's in a market or a property.

News flash: short-term rental investing isn't "passive income," no matter what the IRS says. That four-to-five-time return over traditional rentals? It takes work—revenue management, pricing strategy, marketing, listing optimization, guest communication. You can't just snap your fingers and make it happen. In order to make important decisions, you need to be all-in on markets that you are going to continue to have an interest in. If your interest in either the market or the property cannot be sustained, the property will not yield financial success.

It's also easy to get lost in research, so how many markets should you examine? Start with three to five—no more, no less. Then, narrow it down to one priority market. Pick places that genuinely interest you! My wife and I love lakes, mountains, and national parks. That's why we invested in Banner Elk, North Carolina, with its beautiful mountain climate and two ski resorts. After buying our first place there three years ago, we took family ski lessons that Christmas and fell in love with it. Three months later, we were buying in Whitefish, Montana.

Our passion for these areas kept growing. We added

a luxury condo near Glacier National Park and then that $3,000,000, five-acre property with two houses and a pond that I mentioned earlier. I stocked that pond with rainbow and cutthroat trout.

We didn't stop there—we bought a ski-in, ski-out condo at Whitefish Mountain Resort. We have beach properties because we love the ocean and a lake property near Nashville because we love being on the water. That one's another super property—it has twelve bedrooms and sleeps thirty-eight.

See the pattern? When you invest in markets you're genuinely interested in, you'll pay more attention and have the drive to turn properties into Super Properties. That enthusiasm isn't just about enjoyment—it's about commitment to success.

FINDING YOUR BUY BOX

While interest in the market is important, there are, of course, many other factors involved in market selection—putting them together is where the idea of the "buy box" comes in.

A buy box is the criteria and limitations that you use to target the right property for you. For example, if you have a $400,000 to $500,000 purchase budget and $75,000 in cash, you can't be looking at beach properties and think you're going to buy beachfront or tier two. Your buy box should be focused on mountain markets or lake markets. They will have lower land value costs and entry fees when making that next acquisition.

You hear a lot about markets being saturated, and yes, some are. But most aren't—they just have segments that are saturated by bedroom count. There's not an entire market that's saturated from one bedroom to eight or ten bedrooms. It's typically going to be those middle-range three-, four-, and five-bedroom properties where the general population has been investing. But you also have to look at the quality. Are they just vanilla boxes with Amazon and Ikea furniture, or are they actually *designed* properties?

Take Asheville, North Carolina. Right now, there's some saturation in those bigger four-, five-, and six-bedroom properties with $200,000–$300,000 designs. There's a lady there named Ishita Lalan—she's one of the best designers in the industry. In 2024, she designed about forty properties in that market. If you're going into that space, you need proximity to downtown Asheville or Biltmore, but you'll also have to level up your design. You can't just put in Rooms to Go furniture, without murals and amenities, and expect a return.

That's why we use the Super Property Grader, which I've given you access to. You look at your bedroom count—maybe you're focusing on two- and three-bedroom properties in

Sevierville and Pigeon Forge—and grade the top ten properties. We'll get deeper into the process later, but this is how we identify sub-markets and avoid saturation before we even look at specific properties.

FINAL THOUGHT

One last thing to remember: At some point, you will need a pre-qualification letter. That means having a relationship with a bank. You might not use them for the final loan, but you need that banking relationship to get pre-qualified when submitting offers. We'll dive deeper into this in chapter 8, when we discuss how to make offers.

CHAPTER 3

THE FOUR PILLARS OF INVESTING

Let's be honest—one of the main reasons you're looking at short-term rentals is to magnify your cash flow, but that's only one component of why someone gets into real estate investing. There are actually four pillars—and therefore, four reasons—to investing in any real estate deal: Cash Flow, Appreciation, Debt Paydown, and Tax Benefits. Keeping these in mind, I have tailored these four pillars so that one supports the other.

PILLAR #1: CASH FLOW

When I conduct coaching calls or work with my Inner Circle and mastermind members, cash flow is one of the things we talk about constantly. Simply put, cash flow is the money you actually put in your pocket each year from your investment— after paying all expenses. That includes your mortgage, property taxes, insurance, utilities, maintenance, supplies, and management fees (whether you're managing it yourself or paying someone else).

Remember my first business venture, the T-shirt business? I sold shirts for $20, and after paying $10 for the shirt itself, $10 went into my pocket. That $10 profit was my cash flow. The same thing applies here, just bigger numbers.

Many of you may be moving from long-term to short-term rentals, so let me help you evaluate where you stand right now.

First, let's talk about *return on equity*. *Equity* is the difference between what your property is worth and what you still owe on it—basically, the wealth you've built through appreciation and loan paydown.

As your portfolio grows, that equity becomes a powerful tool. It gives you options: to refinance, reposition, or reinvest. It opens up leverage opportunities that can massively accelerate your path to wealth—but only if you understand how to use it.

Throughout this book, you'll hear me toss out terms like *equity*, *gross*, *net*, and *payback*. While they're fairly straightforward, it's easy to get overwhelmed when you're stepping into a new industry. So let's define them quickly:

- *Gross* refers to your total revenue before any expenses. This is the top-line number on your income report—everything your property brings in before costs.
- *Net* is what you actually keep. It's your profit after deducting all operating expenses, utilities, management fees, taxes, and so on.
- *Payback* is the period of time it takes to earn back your initial cash investment. Not the loan. Not the equity. I'm talking about how long it takes to put the money you spent on the down payment, closing costs, and furnishings back into your pocket from the property's cash flow.

Now, here's the standard I want you to aim for:

Set a goal of achieving a full net return on your equity within eight years or less.

If it takes longer than eight years to get that money back, it's not a great investment.

Here's what I mean: Let's say you have $200,000 in equity, and you're netting $20,000 a year on $70,000 gross.

That's a ten-year payback—which means it's not a high-performing asset. That capital is locked up and underperforming. You're sitting on money that could be earning way more elsewhere.

Let me put it another way: Imagine I show up at your house with a duffel bag containing $200,000 in cold hard cash. I set it on your kitchen table and give you a choice:

1. Take the $200,000 and hand over your property—free and clear. I'll pay off the mortgage, and you walk away.
2. Or keep making $20,000 a year in net cash flow.

Let's say you bought a long-term rental property a few years ago. Over time, the *value of the property has gone up significantly*—maybe you bought it for $300,000, and now it's worth $500,000. That $200,000 difference is *your equity* (minus what you still owe on the mortgage).

Stay with me here. While the value of your property has grown fast, your *cash flow*—the money you're actually putting in your pocket each year after expenses—is still relatively low. Maybe you're only netting $10,000 to $12,000 per year.

That means you're sitting on hundreds of thousands of dollars in equity, but the property is only generating a modest return. At that pace, it will take you *twenty years* just to earn back what the property is worth in cash flow. That's what we mean by a *twenty-year payback*.

So, what's the issue? The *equity has grown faster than the income*, and that's not efficient.

You made a great buy. The market appreciated. But now your capital is *locked in* a property that isn't giving you strong returns.

That's why repositioning matters. If you sold or refinanced that property, pulled out that equity, and moved it into a high-performing short-term rental? You could dramatically increase your cash flow and shorten your payback window.

Put simply: *You're rich on paper—but your money isn't working hard enough.*

How do you know if it's time to reposition? Perform a *return on equity audit.*

A return on equity audit is a simple process to determine whether your current property is still the best use of your capital. We use these audits to evaluate whether it's time to reposition a property—either by refinancing or selling and reinvesting—so we can maximize cash flow and return.

Here's how it works:

1. Figure out your payoff amount (check your mortgage statement or call your lender)
2. Check Zillow for your property's estimated value (reduce it by 5–6 percent, because it's always inflated)
3. Factor in closing costs (usually about 10 percent)

4. Evaluate what you could reinvest (That's the true equity after expenses—the amount you can actually use to level up.)

For example:

- You owe: $300,000
- Zillow (after the 5–6 percent reduction) says: $500,000
- The delta (sometimes presented as the symbol Δ, or difference between what's owed and Zillow): $200,000
- Closing costs (approximately 10 percent of sale price): $50,000
- Final amount available for you to reinvest: $150,000

Property Is Worth
$500,000

– You Owe
$300,000

– 10% Closing Costs
=

$150,000 to Reinvest

That $150,000 can then level you up into a $500,000 property, where you were previously in a $200,000 or $250,000 property.

When you reposition into the right property, apply the strategies in this book, and stay consistent with your pricing and marketing, you're no longer aiming for average returns. You're positioned to outperform the market.

Tools like AirDNA and STR Insights offer solid benchmarks, but my approach is designed to go beyond those. Not just into the top 25 percent, but well past the 90th percentile. I routinely perform 40 to 50 percent above that line.

This doesn't happen by accident. It comes from optimizing revenue, using dynamic pricing effectively, and making sure every part of the listing—from the photos and descriptions to the amenities and guest experience—is built to convert.

The result? Higher gross revenue, stronger net cash flow, and a dramatically shorter payback period.

I'm not in this to wait twelve to fifteen years for a property to pay itself off. My target is four to six years. If I'm looking at five or six years, I'm already thinking about selling and reinvesting in something that will perform better.

I don't want 100 properties. Right now, I own about a dozen. My goal isn't to stack doors; it's to *maximize the performance* of each one. I don't need 50 or 100 to generate serious income.

What I need—and what I focus on—is a small portfolio of Super Properties and a system that works.

This is a key part of the 250 Plan. My average hold time for a short-term rental? Just under three and a half years. Why? Because equity, especially during and post-COVID, has been growing so fast. You start small—like that $375,000 property— and level up to $1 million or even $3 million.

PILLAR #2: APPRECIATION

If you own your own home, you're probably already familiar with appreciation. Assets are usually classified as appreciating or depreciating. Real estate is typically considered an appreciating asset because usually, property values increase; something like a car or boat would be considered a depreciating asset because even though both are investments of significant amounts of money, they usually do not retain or gain monetary value over time.

When underwriting a property, you will need to look at the appreciation rate—but not just the overall market rate. It's going to be completely different for a $2 million property versus a $400,000 property.

If you're buying that $2 million property, I want you to look specifically at:

- Properties in that same price range
- Same bedroom count
- Similar acreage
- Comparable features

Your agent should be able to get this information from the National Association of Realtors (NAR). Here's what to look at:

- Appreciation rates for the past five years, unless those include 2021 and 2020
- Skip 2021 and 2020 (those COVID numbers will never be seen again)
- Go back to 2019 and 2018
- Average those five years together

Want to take it two steps further? Here's what I do:

1. Go to the planning commission to see what developments are coming
2. Contact the Chamber of Commerce to understand what's happening in the market

Let me give you a real example: I just invested heavily in Whitefish, Montana, because I know what's happening in that luxury and ultra-luxury space. I purchased a $3 million property that's getting 7.5 percent appreciation. I'm not really smart (remember, I dropped out of college), but let's do some easy math:

7.5% of $3 million = $225,000 a year in appreciation

- That alone roughly covers my mortgage
- It doesn't help with cash flow directly (that's why we still need the Super Property Grader and Proforma tools)
- This property is projected to net about $125,000 annually in cash flow
- When you combine that with the 7.5 percent appreciation, you're looking at $350,000 in total annual gain

Now, if you don't have to live off that cash flow, you can really start accelerating your wealth building. But remember—appreciation is just one pillar. It works together with all the other pillars to create true wealth through the 250 Plan, which brings us to . . .

PILLAR #3: DEBT PAYDOWN

If you've started using my Proforma tool, you've noticed two sections in the bottom left-hand corner for financing options: 20-year and 30-year terms. The following is my advice for debt paydown.

You can do the 30-year term, but if you don't have to live off your investments, I strongly advise making extra principal payments out of your profit. Why? Because paying down debt faster lets us reposition quicker.

Let me explain why.

If you've ever been a Limited Partner (LP) in a real estate syndication, you've seen how the General Partner (GP) operates. (And if you haven't, here's a quick breakdown: The LP is a passive investor, putting money in but not managing the deal. The GP is the one running the project, making decisions, and earning a bigger cut for taking on the work and risk.)

The GP's goal is to maximize returns and get the LP's money back as quickly as possible. They typically:

- Reposition the asset through upgrades and better operations
- Refinance or sell to extract equity
- Pay back the LP and take their percentage of the upside

That same principle applies here. The faster you can pay down debt and increase equity, the faster you can reposition. Whether that's through a cash-out refi or a full sale, repositioning lets you level up and scale your portfolio far faster than someone who just rides out a 30-year mortgage.

I bring this same mentality to short-term rentals—something almost no one else does. Everyone else is legacy, traditional buy-and-hold. Not me. I want to buy and reposition as quickly as possible, because that's how you accelerate the 250 Plan.

Here's a real example from my portfolio of a beach house I just sold that was appreciating at 8 percent:

- Owned for 2.5 years
- Purchase price: $980,000
- Seller concession received: $40,000
- Total investment (or basis): $940,000

Note: A s*eller concession* isn't a reduction in price. You're still buying the property at full value—$980,000 in this case. But the seller agrees to give you a certain amount of money at closing (in this case, $40,000) that you can use toward renovations, closing costs, or even to buy down your interest rate.

What is basis?

Basis is your total financial investment in the property,

including the purchase price minus any seller concessions plus any capital improvements or significant closing costs. In this case, with a $40,000 seller concession, my basis was $940,000 + closing costs and improvements.

- Sale price: $1.7 million
- Equity gain (or profit): $665,000

What did I do with that money?

- Paid $2.8 million for a Montana property
- Invested an additional $200,000 for rehab and design

Now, you might be wondering—why sell a property appreciating at 8 percent to buy one at 7.5 percent? Because I went from a $1.7 million property to a nearly $3 million property. Think about that delta: 7.5 percent on $3 million is about another $100,000 a year in appreciation.

That's the beauty of the 250 Plan. After that $3 million property, I went right back to:

- A $559,000 property
- And just went under contract for a $395,000 property that will give me 35 percent cash-on-cash

That's where the numbers really start compounding.

Cash-on-cash return, by the way, is one of my favorite performance metrics—it tells you how much money you're making based on how much cash you actually invested. If you put in $100,000 and earn $35,000 in net profit annually, that's a 35 percent cash-on-cash return. Not theoretical value—real, usable income.

And the way you finance these deals matters just as much.

Personally, I love 20-year amortizations. Sure, the monthly payments are higher than a 30-year mortgage, but you're paying off the principal faster—and that accelerates your equity build-up. More equity means more repositioning power.

Amortization just refers to the way your loan is structured to pay down over time. A shorter amortization equals faster debt payoff and less interest paid over the life of the loan.

Now, if you're not in a position to do a 20-year term? Go for 30 years—but make extra principal payments out of your profits. That's how you collapse the timeline, pay off debt faster, and free up equity to move up again.

If this seems to accelerate at a fast pace, you are absolutely right. When you understand how to use debt strategically, you can dramatically impact your cash flow and build wealth faster than you ever thought possible.

PILLAR #4: TAX BENEFITS

This is where the magic of short-term rentals *really* comes into play. Beyond the cash flow and appreciation, one of the biggest perks is how much money you can save on taxes—especially with a couple of items known as *cost-segregation study* and *accelerated depreciation*.

Let me break that down in simple terms.

Normally, when you buy a property, the IRS lets you write off a little bit of it every year to account for things wearing down over time. That's called depreciation, and it usually gets spread out over 27.5 years. Each year, then, you get a small tax break.

But we're not here for small tax breaks. We want the big stuff up front.

That's where a *cost-segregation study* comes in. It's basically a fancy report done by an expert cost segregation engineer that looks at all the different parts of your property—like flooring, appliances, cabinets, and even the landscaping—and says, "Hey, this stuff doesn't last 27.5 years. We can write off a big chunk of this way faster based on its actual depreciation schedule."

That's what we call *accelerated depreciation*—it means you get to claim a lot more of those tax savings right away, instead of waiting decades.

Here's what that looked like for my $3 million property in Montana:

- I paid $4,000 for a cost-segregation study
- It unlocked around $485,000 in depreciation
- The majority of that depreciation is applied in the year you purchase the property

Now, if I sell the property within the first five years of ownership, the IRS will want that depreciation back.

Why five years? Because if I sell the property before that, the IRS might ask for some of that money back. That's called "recapture," and it's something I always plan for just in case.

So when I look at what I'm making every year on that property, here's the full picture:

- Cash Flow (after expenses): $125,000
- Appreciation (7.5 percent of $3M): $225,000
- Year One Tax Savings: $485,000

Altogether, that's nearly $835,000 of real financial benefit every year from one property.

And here's the best part—those tax savings? They help me keep more of the money I already earned. That means I have more to reinvest into other properties . . . which fuels my next deal.

Even now, while bonus depreciation is temporarily down to 40 percent, it's still one of the best tools in the game. And if it goes back to 100 percent? Even better. Either way, this is one of the biggest reasons why short-term rentals can build wealth so quickly when you know how to play the game.

* * *

When you combine all Four Pillars and stay steadfast to them, using the Super Property Grader to evaluate opportunities and the Proforma to underwrite deals—always adding in that JICYFU (just in case you f*ck up) 20 percent delta—you'll be able to execute the 250 Plan in less than five years. That's if you're investing smartly, of course.

Let me be clear: Don't get greedy and start buying only big properties. There's a reason I have a diversified portfolio of motels, single-family homes, and condos spread across multiple markets nationwide.

Just like a well-oiled stock portfolio, we don't want all our eggs in one basket. The Four Pillars protect us, guide us, and shape our portfolio to maximize the 250 Plan for the most returns with the fewest number of properties.

CHAPTER 4

THE 250 PLAN

Now that we've covered the four pillars of investing, which are the core of the 250 Plan, let me break it down for you from a mindset standpoint.

START SMALL

With the 250 Plan, you start small and level up. The typical progression looks like this:

- Property #1: $400,000–$500,000 range
- Property #2: $600,000–$800,000
- Property #3: $800,000–$1 million
- Property #4: $1 million–$2 million
- Property #5: $1,675,000

The 250 Plan

Reposition
(Between property 2 and 4)

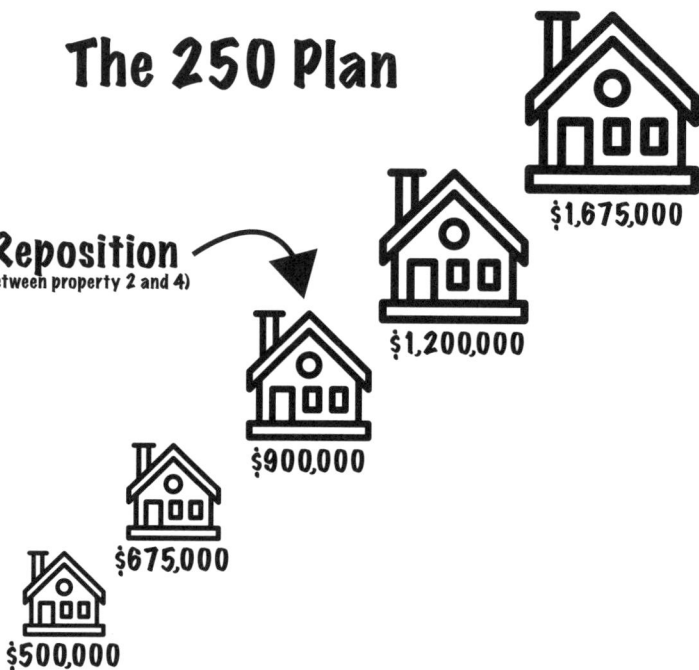

$1,675,000

$1,200,000

$900,000

$675,000

$500,000

The goal? Five properties, each producing about $50,000 in net income. And remember, this is cyclical; each time you complete the cycle, you'll start over. That's how you keep scaling. That's how you build wealth.

Let me give you a real example from my own journey.

I bought my first property, Bella Vista, for $629,000. I held it for about two years. During that time, I accelerated debt paydown using the property's cash flow and built equity through appreciation and tax advantages. That one property gave me the capital ($450,000) I needed to make my next big move.

From there, I split the proceeds:

- $300,000 went toward a lot in Gulf Shores, where I built a $900,000 beach property now worth $2 million.
- The remaining $150,000 helped me purchase a $495,000 lake house.

Eighteen months later, I sold that lake house for $725,000—then rolled that equity into a larger $800,000 property with enough left over for a $125,000 renovation.

And that's the beauty of the 250 Plan.

Each property helps you acquire the next. You reposition early and often to climb the ladder faster.

It's not always about going bigger, either. After purchasing a $3 million property in Montana, I immediately went back down to a $559,000 condo. Why? Because I had just completed a cycle. The goal isn't to grow in a straight line—it's to cycle equity, improve your position, and repeat the process.

If I were writing this in 2020 or 2021, I'd tell you to hold and refinance at 2.93 percent. But with today's 7–8 percent interest rates, that doesn't pencil. Refinancing adds thousands in monthly debt service that crushes your Proforma.

That's why we reposition. That's why we sell. That's why we move faster.

READY TO LAUNCH

So how do we launch the 250 Plan? It depends on how much (or even how little) money you have to begin. If you have no money, start with *cohosting*—that's where you would have a more hands-on role in the actual management of the property. We'll discuss that in more detail, along with Fast Money, Medium Money, and Slow Money in the next chapter, but for now, just know that yes, it's possible to start with a low- or no-money down payment.

If you have $100,000, start looking at properties with a

price point of around $450,000.

Here's one idea of how the numbers can work:

Starting Position

- You have $100,000 in capital
- You negotiate a $40,000 concession

Annual Returns Breakdown

1. Cash Flow = $45,000
   (Annual net income from the property)

2. Appreciation (5 percent) = $20,000
   (On a $450,000 property: 5 percent × $450K = $22,500, but let's round down to keep it simple)

3. Accelerated Debt Paydown = $10,000
   (Extra principal payments reducing loan balance, increasing equity)

4. Concession (year 1 benefit) = $40,000
   (Immediate value captured at closing—reduces your out-of-pocket investment)

Total Wealth Created in Year One

- $45,000 (Cash Flow)
- $20,000 (Appreciation)
- $10,000 (Debt Paydown)
- $40,000 (Concession)

= $115,000 Total Wealth Created in Year One

Your initial $100,000 turned into $115,000 of total benefit (including realized and unrealized gains) in just one year, under these assumptions. That's an immediate 15+ percent gain on top of breaking even, which puts you solidly on the path for accelerating your journey through the 250 Plan.

$450,000 Purchase Price

$45,000 Net Profit Per Year

+ $20,000 (5% Appreciation)

+$10,000 Debt Paydown

+$40,000 Seller Concession
=

$115,000 Wealth Created in Year One

Repositioning Can Happen at Any Time— but Timing It Well Accelerates the 250 Plan

You *can* reposition at any point in your journey. Whether it's after your first property or your fifth, there's no strict rule. But here's the thing: repositioning is most powerful when you've started stacking all the pillars—cash flow, appreciation, debt paydown, and tax benefits—plus a well-negotiated seller concession.

That's what I mean when I talk about *stacking*. You're not relying on just one stream of return. You're combining all four wealth-building pillars and then adding the bonus of a seller concession to compound your returns.

Here's Where Most People Go Wrong

They either hold on too long and let equity sit idle, or they reposition too early without having optimized their property's performance.

When we talk about *repositioning between properties two and four*, that's not a hard rule—it's just the sweet spot. By this point, you've likely:

- Proven your ability to cash flow
- Benefited from at least some appreciation

- Paid down part of the loan principal
- Captured early-stage tax benefits (especially if you did a cost seg)
- Positioned yourself for your next move with experience and leverage

This is when the compounding power of the 250 Plan kicks in.

Because now, you're not just moving from one property to another. You're trading up into something better—more profitable, more unique, more optimized—using the momentum you've built.

Repositioning is your tool to scale without adding unnecessary properties. It's how you go from *good* to *great* in fewer steps.

Does this mean you invest anywhere? Absolutely not. But if you have marketing and revenue management skills and you find a unique property, you can execute the 250 Plan in any market.

Think about it like a real estate syndication. The goal in syndications is always to reposition quickly—refinance, sell, or otherwise return investor capital early. But here's the difference: in multifamily and commercial real estate, investors measure performance using capitalization rate ("cap rates") and Net Operating Income (NOI).

Let's break that down:

- *NOI* is your property's income after operating expenses but before your mortgage. That includes things like taxes, insurance, maintenance, and utilities.
- *Cap rate* is your NOI divided by the property's purchase price or current value. It tells you what percentage return you're getting *based on the property's value.*

Example: If your property earns $50,000 in NOI and costs $500,000, your cap rate is 10 percent.

This is the standard in commercial real estate—because cap rates drive property value. Increase your NOI, and you force appreciation.

But in single-family homes and short-term rentals, property values are based on comparable sales (comps), not cap rates. While NOI is still helpful in evaluating performance, it doesn't influence your appraised value in the same way.

Keep It Simple, Keep It Straight

This can get technical fast, so I want to bring it back to your priorities. The order matters:

1. **Cash Flow:** Make sure the property covers its expenses and pays you.
2. **Appreciation:** Look for markets where you expect 5–10 percent annual growth.
3. **Debt Paydown**: I prefer 20-year amortizations when possible. If you choose a 30-year loan, make extra principal payments with your profit.
4. **Tax Benefits**: Take advantage of tools like cost segregation and short-term rental tax loopholes. Just remember, *depreciation is recaptured if you sell within five years*, so I amortize that benefit accordingly.

I created the 250 Plan out of necessity because I didn't know what I was doing when I started. Remember, *all experts start as beginners*. You're investing in yourself, and by the end of this book, you will be a better investor. No question about it. And the 250 Plan works; thousands of my members have executed it successfully, even with no money down.

CHAPTER 5

STARTING WITH NO MONEY

If you don't have any money but you still want to get into the short-term rental game, there is a way to do that—you'll just start down a different path. Yes, there is a legit way to break into this industry starting with no money down, but let's be clear: you're not going to walk in and buy a property with *nothing*. You're just not walking into it with legal tender.

Most investors—friends, family, or otherwise—won't give you money unless you've built a proven track record. I generally don't recommend taking money from people you care about unless you're 100 percent confident you can deliver a return on a clearly defined timeline. You'll need to take a smarter route.

ENTER FAST, MEDIUM, AND SLOW MONEY

Before we go further, I want to introduce a concept that will shape how you build wealth inside and outside of real estate: Fast, Medium, and Slow Money.

- **Fast Money:** This is income you can generate within a few weeks or months. Think flipping a property or setting up a cohosting deal that pays you within thirty days.
- **Medium Money:** Revenue that starts flowing in three to twelve months. This could be cohosting deals that start with a setup fee and ramp into monthly income or short-term flip projects.
- **Slow Money:** These are your long-term plays— buying properties and waiting for appreciation, net cash flow, tax benefits, and equity to build. Think three to five years or more before seeing your full return.

THE SMARTER WAY TO START: COHOSTING

If you don't have the capital to invest upfront, cohosting is the best way to break into the industry. Cohosting is similar to property management, but more transparent and hands-on. As a cohost, you:

- Manage the property
- Handle guest communication
- Oversee cleaners and handymen
- Optimize pricing and revenue
- Improve listings with better marketing and staging

Cohosting falls into both the Fast and Medium Money categories. That's what makes it so powerful for beginners. It costs nothing to start, gives you experience, and starts generating income quickly—unlike buying a home and waiting years for a return.

Again—cohosting costs *nothing* to get started, and it's the safest way to gain experience while making money. The hardest part? Landing your *first* client.

That's what I want to focus on right now. You're not going to have the experience; you're not going to be able to conduct revenue management. That's why the first thing you want to do is build a case study.

STEP 1: BUILD A CASE STUDY (EVEN WITHOUT CLIENTS)

Without experience, you can't just walk up to a property owner and pitch your cohosting services. You need *proof* that you know what you're doing. That means building a case study.

How to Build a Case Study Without Clients

1. **Choose the Right Market**
- Pick a market that interests you but also has high-value properties.
- Avoid low-revenue markets—no disrespect to Topeka, Kansas, but you'll make more in places like Scottsdale (Arizona), Outer Banks (North Carolina), Gulf Shores (Alabama), or Destin (Florida).
- Educate yourself on that market's short-term rental landscape for a couple of weeks.

2. Analyze Underperforming Properties

- Use tools like my **Super Property Grader** and **Proforma** to score properties.
- Look at competitor listings and find ones that are *underperforming*.
- Identify quick, high-impact improvements (better photos, updated bedding, added amenities, staging tweaks).

3. Offer to Work for Free (Temporarily)

- Approach an owner with a weak property (low Super Score).
- Show them how you can improve their revenue.
- Manage and optimize their listing for sixty to ninety days *for free* to prove your value.
- This isn't charity—it's a strategic investment in your credibility.

If you can take a failing-grade listing (one that would receive a *D* or *F*) and turn it into a high-performing one, you now have a golden marketing asset. That owner may likely convert into a paying client, but regardless, you'll have the *data* and *proof* to bring in more customers.

STEP 2: USE YOUR CASE STUDY
TO GET PAYING CLIENTS

Now that you have results, it's time to leverage them.

1. Use Social Proof to Attract Owners
- Get testimonials from your first client.
- Create a case study showing the before-and-after numbers.

2. Engage in Local Facebook Groups
- Find groups where short-term rental owners and guests hang out.
- Post about your results: *Hey, is anyone looking to make more money with their Airbnb? I just helped an owner increase their revenue by 30 percent—happy to share how.*
- Offer a free forty-five-minute Zoom training to educate potential clients.

3. Run a No-Strings-Attached Zoom Call
- Teach three or four key items, like revenue management, listing optimization, and staging.
- No sales pitch. Just *give value.*

- At the end, some owners will say, "This is great, but I don't have time for it. Can you just do it for me?"
- *Boom.* New paying clients.

STEP 3: SCALE YOUR BUSINESS

Once you have paying clients, you're in business. But don't stop there.

Research Underperforming Properties
- Use AirDNA or STR Insights to find poorly managed listings.
- Cross-reference them with Google Maps and Street View to pinpoint locations.

Reach Out with a Data-Driven Pitch
- Show them how they're losing money.
- Explain exactly how you'll increase their revenue.

Rinse & Repeat
- Every successful cohosting deal adds to your credibility.
- With enough clients, you're making $100K–$200K a year.

- After twelve to thirteen months, you'll have enough capital to buy your own rental property.

STOP WASTING TIME ON OUTDATED STRATEGIES

Forget the old-school methods people are pushing—like sending five hundred direct-mail pieces that no one opens. That's slow, expensive, and ineffective. Instead, position yourself as the *expert* in your market, give value first, and let the clients come to *you*.

If you follow this process, you're on the fast track to a six-figure cohosting business. And if you want to take it to the next level, follow the QR code below to check out my Cohosting Masterclass—it includes contracts, business plans, and a step-by-step guide to executing everything we just covered.

CHAPTER 6

CHOOSING YOUR MARKET

Now that you know how to prepare to identify your first market and which avenue to take in order to buy your first property, it's time to dive in and select three to five markets that interest you for investment.

Let's start by discussing some essential tools that will help you with this process. My preferred tool is STR Insights, available at STRinsights.com. It's created by my friend and mastermind member, Kenny Bedwell, who wrote the foreword to this book. He is also the number-one property picker I mentioned earlier. Now I don't necessarily recommend hiring someone like Kenny for your *first* investment, especially if you're working with a small budget; that said, you should have your budget determined before starting your market selection. There will be plenty of time for you to find your own "Kenny" later, if you so choose.

DON'T FOLLOW THE HERD

First and foremost, please avoid turning to social media to find the best markets for investment. Even if you join my Build Short Term Rental Wealth Facebook group, other group members will only tell you about their successes in their specific locations, without providing crucial context. You won't know if they're in Gulf Shores with a property five blocks from the beach, if they paid $200,000, if they bought it in 2015, or if they have amenities, like a pool or beach views. *Context is essential*, which is why you need to start with your budget set and financials ready.

I highly recommend using STR Insights because it provides one particularly valuable piece of data during your search: gross ROI. When you search for a location like Asheville, North Carolina, it shows you the gross ROI percentage based on bedroom count for average two-bedroom, three-bedroom, four-bedroom properties, and so on.

This gross ROI gives you a comparative framework. For instance, if you see a 15 percent gross ROI in Asheville, 13 percent in Sevierville, and 11 percent in Blue Ridge, Georgia, and you're interested in the Blue Ridge mountain area, then Asheville, North Carolina, might be your best starting point.

Why is it so crucial to analyze by bedroom count? Because

different sizes of properties generate varying gross ROIs and revenue. One key principle I've learned in my investing career is that lower entry price points typically yield higher cash-on-cash returns. Let me offer you an example.

For a $300,000 property, I aim for a 30–35 percent cash-on-cash return. However, with a $1.5 million property, achieving such returns becomes challenging, and they typically range from 15–18 percent if they're solid investments. I never accept anything under 10 percent. The rule of thumb is, smaller properties offer higher cash-on-cash returns; larger properties provide higher cash flow but lower cash-on-cash returns.

What do I mean by *cash-on-cash return*? To illustrate: If you invest $200,000 in cash into a property and net $100,000, that's a 50 percent cash-on-cash return because you're getting 50 percent back in your first year.

I personally look for a four-year return, aiming for 25 percent, regardless of price point. Using the same numbers, I would expect to net $50,000 each year from a $200,000 cash investment to recoup my initial investment in four years.

My approach differs due to my years of experience. I excel at property selection, revenue management, market and amenity analysis, competition assessment, off-platform marketing, and listing optimization. These skills—which I'll cover later in the book—are crucial for reaching the elite level and becoming a top-one-percenter like me. I want you to develop these skills, particularly in analyzing properties and markets, but you need to grasp the fundamentals first.

Cash-on-Cash Calculation

$100,000 Net Profit
/
$200,000 Cash Investment
=
50% Cash on Cash

$200,000 Cash Investment
with $50,000 a Year in Net Profit
= 4 Years to get back cash investment

SUBMARKETS

When using STR Insights, I first examine submarkets.

Submarkets are smaller, more specific areas within a larger destination or metro that often have unique demand drivers, guest behaviors, or pricing dynamics. These aren't always official city limits—they might be a neighborhood, a popular village, a ski resort base area, or even a particular stretch of coastline.

For example, Scottsdale is considered the main market—but Old Town Scottsdale is a submarket. Gulf Shores is the market, but West Beach or Lagoon Pass could be submarkets. In the Smoky Mountains, you've got Gatlinburg, Pigeon Forge, and Sevierville—each with their own distinct submarket data and pricing performance.

Submarkets are critical because they let you:

- Compare apples to apples (you don't want to benchmark a downtown condo against a mountain cabin thirty minutes away).
- Understand what's driving top performance within a focused area.
- Spot opportunity where supply is low, but demand is high.

When I'm evaluating properties, I always want to make sure the Super Property Grader and revenue data are specific to the submarket, not just the overall region. That level of precision is what separates good investors from great ones.

Every market has stronger and weaker submarkets. Take the Smoky Mountains, for example. You have three main submarkets: Pigeon Forge, Gatlinburg, and Sevierville (all located in Tennessee). Within these, you'll find secondary submarkets. As I write this, I would avoid areas like Wears Valley, located about five to ten miles from downtown Pigeon Forge. It's oversaturated in almost all bedroom counts, and the distance from both Pigeon Forge and the Smoky Mountains is too far for most who want to visit the area. Instead, I focus on different submarkets *within the three primary areas*, analyzing which bedroom counts perform best.

If I were investing in the Smokies as of this writing, I'd target one- or two-bedroom properties, particularly one-bedrooms with pools, as they're performing similarly to larger units. Why pay more for a two- or three-bedroom when a one-bedroom can match or outperform them in terms of gross revenue return? Especially considering you'd pay almost double for a three-bedroom.

Currently, you can find a one-bedroom with a pool for around $400,000—sometimes even $350,000 if you discover a great deal—that can generate $100,000–$225,000 annually. Meanwhile, many three-bedrooms with pools might only generate $80,000–$90,000 per year. This demonstrates why market breakdown to submarket and bedroom count analysis is crucial.

In places like Asheville, North Carolina, you'll also want to examine the gross ROI returns by bedroom count—whether it's two-bedroom, three-bedroom, four-bedroom, or whatever suits your budget. Instead of purchasing one home with five-bedrooms at $800,000, consider whether you might be better off buying two two-bedrooms, or even three one-bedrooms, to maximize your returns.

Remember, however, that when you add more doors (i.e., properties), managing three $250,000 properties versus one $800,000 property typically requires three times the effort in terms of guest management, turnovers, cleaning, linen replacement, and other operational tasks. Consider this time investment when searching for markets and properties.

TRAFFIC DRIVERS

My standard approach when identifying a market begins with identifying traffic drivers. These are markets that are consistently attracting visitors year-round and are usually identified by strong tourism data, major attractions, or recurring events that bring in predictable demand.

When we think about markets that are traffic drivers, I'm guessing your mind automatically went to the beach. That is almost a reflex, frankly. Beach markets are straightforward, practically a given. Beaches are practically synonymous with "vacation home," or "vacation," even if you're primarily a mountain and lake person like I am. Our mind just sort of travels there when we think about a vacation, even if we ultimately decide to tour Europe or go camping in the woods. A beach, therefore, is an obvious primary traffic driver.

As I mentioned, I invest in Gulf Shores, Alabama, instead of areas like 30A, Destin, or similar locations in Florida. The traffic patterns differ significantly among the Seaside area, the Seacraft area in central 30A, and Gulf Shores.

One distinctive feature I discovered in Gulf Shores is its off-season events, which are what I like to call *compression events*. They typically last a weekend or day and are different from market seasonality.

These events—cheerleading competitions, soccer tournaments, dance competitions, the Boots in the Sand Festival in Gulf Shores, and NCAA championships—occur in a very specific, compressed timeframe and provide excellent short-term spikes but don't transform winter (for example) into peak season. Sunday through Thursday demand remains low during these periods, requiring strategic off-platform marketing and revenue management to secure bookings.

These types of events occur less frequently in Destin and even less in 30A or Panama City Beach, resulting in varying season lengths. Gulf Shores benefits from two major sports complexes; one is located in Orange Beach and another in Foley, both in Alabama. These venues host soccer tournaments with 3,000–4,000 participants almost every weekend. The convention center in Orange Beach regularly hosts cheerleading and dance competitions, drawing thousands of participants throughout fall and winter. These compression events aren't as common in the Destin, Panama City Beach, and 30A markets, which factors into my market comparison. These sorts of details aren't necessarily going to show up on a property listing, so it's worth the extra digging when you're considering a market.

While peak rates during spring break, fall break, and the Memorial Day to Labor Day period are achievable anywhere, the *real* profit comes from off-season bookings. That's why I focus on traffic drivers and whatever they may yield. When I declined to invest in Hot Springs, Arkansas, I was actually turning down one of the few markets nationwide with four legitimate traffic drivers:

- Lake Hamilton, which extends nearly into downtown
- A casino
- A national park about a mile and a half from downtown
- A major horse track operating six months annually with off-site betting facilities

These four substantial traffic drivers in a compact market create significant financial opportunity. You can leverage these year-round attractions effectively.

Most strong markets typically have one or two traffic drivers, often seasonal. And remember, seasonal marketability is different from compression events, even if those events occur annually.

Consider Snowshoe, West Virginia—it has the Snowshoe Ski Resort and little else. While some promote summer mountain biking, ski resort markets primarily depend on winter seasons. This applies to Beech Mountain, Sugar Mountain in North Carolina, West View in West Virginia, and even premium locations like Aspen and Breckenridge—summer simply can't compete with winter ski season revenue. And since you can't control the snowfall, that can easily disrupt your 250 Plan.

With lake properties, I specifically target Southern locations due to their extended favorable weather conditions. At places like Smith Lake near Huntsville and Birmingham, Alabama, we see strong business during March and April for spring break, as temperatures rise and water warms. The season extends through fall—you can swim there until Thanksgiving. Compare this to Lake Norman in North Carolina or lakes near Indianapolis or in Michigan, where swimming season ends much earlier. This extended season, combined with compression events, creates additional revenue opportunities. These are crucial data points to consider when evaluating a market.

PROXIMITY IS CRUCIAL

When analyzing markets, proximity's importance cannot be overstated. Top-performing properties typically have prime locations. In mountain areas, views matter significantly. In beach markets like Panama City Beach, Destin, or Gulf Shores, tier-two properties (one street back from the beach) perform differently based on ocean views. Don't assume similar performance to top-tier properties without matching their view amenities.

The same applies to ski resorts. Newry, Maine, illustrates this well. Many investors have purchased excellent new construction cabins there due to Sunday River Ski Resort. However, properties fifteen to twenty minutes away in Bethel perform below those within five minutes of the resort, especially those with slope views.

Whitefish, Montana, appeals to me because Whitefish Ski Resort provides winter activity to complement summer attractions like fly fishing, hiking, boating, lakes, and Glacier National Park, which draws four million annual visitors. With properly positioned properties near the ski resort, we can capitalize on two full market seasons that amount to about nine to ten months of predictable revenue.

In the Smoky Mountains, you can't effectively leverage Dollywood's traffic if you're twenty minutes away. Visitors prefer staying within a ten- to fifteen-minute drive due to traffic concerns. Similarly, while Wears Valley properties market their Pigeon Forge proximity, traffic can extend drive times from twenty to even forty minutes, making them less marketable.

This is why I emphasize using my Super Property Grader when analyzing submarkets and bedroom counts. Evaluate ten key factors, including location, proximity, photo quality, and amenities across eight to ten properties. While somewhat subjective, this rating system helps compare potential investments against existing successful properties, providing a mathematical framework to assess investment viability and potential peak performance.

THINGS CAN CHANGE

In 2021, Kenny Bedwell shared his first market analysis spreadsheet with my Mastermind group in Gatlinburg, Tennessee, before launching STR Insights.

Among the top one hundred U.S. markets based on gross ROI, Logan, Ohio (Hocking Hills) ranked first, primarily because you could purchase a five- or six-bedroom property for $350,000–$375,000 at that time. Its high ranking stemmed from having a state park nearby, low entry prices, and COVID-driven demand. Fast forward to 2023 and beyond, post-COVID, Logan, Ohio, isn't even in the top *two hundred* markets. While the state park remains an attraction, people aren't constantly seeking outdoor escape like during the pandemic. With just one primary traffic driver, Logan, Ohio, thrived during COVID but isn't an optimal investment location today.

Similarly, Ellijay and Blue Ridge, Georgia, benefited from four or five million Atlanta residents seeking escape during COVID, making them the closest viable destinations. Market conditions have changed significantly, however. Remember that markets and demand patterns shift—they don't maintain consistency indefinitely.

The Smoky Mountains stand out as the most consistent market over the past decade. Even though I don't currently invest there, it has maintained remarkable stability because over 24 million people can reach the park within an eight-hour drive, making it America's most visited national park. In terms of the Smoky Mountains' traffic drivers, there are a few, and they are substantial.

First, there's Dollywood. Second, you have the mountains themselves, offering hiking, rivers, and outdoor activities like whitewater rafting. Third, there's the entertainment district from downtown Pigeon Forge to Gatlinburg's strip. These are substantial traffic drivers—not small festivals or events.

These are the types of indicators you should evaluate when analyzing potential investment markets. I recommend having at least two traffic drivers. Following these guidelines, along with implementing all the strategies discussed in this chapter and using the Super Property Grader and Proforma, will help you mitigate risk and increase your chances of securing a Super Property.

CHAPTER 7

PROPERTY SELECTION AND UNDERWRITING

You've selected your market. Now it's time to get down to the nitty-gritty of selecting your property.

The first step in property selection is identifying something unique about the property. This is where the Super Property Grader comes in. We need to analyze at least eight properties in addition to our target property. I recommend evaluating ten total—your potential property, plus nine others. Your goal is to get a true sense of how your property compares to what's already winning.

During this analysis, we'll examine proximity, location, views, amenities, listing quality, marketability, photo quality, interior, and exterior. We'll rate each of these aspects on a scale of one to ten, starting with the property you're currently considering.

You must be brutally honest in this assessment.

If you let your emotions lead—if you get attached to the view, the kitchen, or that perfect wraparound porch—and start handing out inflated nines and tens, you're sabotaging your own investment. Being genuinely excited about a property is great. In fact, I encourage it. But emotional excitement and objective analysis need to coexist. Interest is fine—bias is the problem.

This process helps to make sure your excitement doesn't blind you from the facts, because we're going to apply the exact same rating system to the other nine properties. Your "dream property" has to hold up under the same scrutiny as all the others. That's how you get a real Super Score—a data-driven comparison that tells you if this investment is truly competitive in your market.

Be sure to stay within the same bedroom count for this analysis so you're comparing apples to apples.

For those wanting to take it to the pro level, I'll share my personal method: If I'm buying a two-bedroom property, I'll run the Super Property Grader through comparable two-bedrooms and get ratings for all ten properties (including my target property). Then I'll level up and perform the same analysis for three-bedrooms. This exemplifies taking those extra steps. Even though I might dominate the two-bedroom category, I want to see how I stack up against the three-bedroom competition. If I can compete there, I know I've found a rock-solid investment.

DETERMINE YOUR INVESTMENT REQUIREMENTS

You see, the Super Property Grader reveals more than just a score. The Super Property Grader gives you the opportunity to discover what's missing in your selected properties and what features are present; these become your post-closing investment requirements.

In mountain or lake properties, for example, you'll likely notice every top-performing property has a hot tub. The second most common amenity is typically a fire pit; not a $600 propane tank version from Home Depot, but a proper wood-burning pit with four to twelve chairs, depending on property size. These amenities will impact your cash-on-cash return if your target property lacks them. This extends beyond hot tubs and fireplaces to include coffee bars, bedroom murals, accent walls, and game rooms—items that make your property stand out in Airbnb listings.

Just a few years ago, when I bought in Banner Elk, the

Smokies already required $50,000 to $100,000 game rooms for top properties, followed by indoor pools costing another hundred thousand or so. In Banner Elk—one of those secondary markets where I recommend investing rather than primary markets—only one property sleeping over fourteen guests had a game room. This allowed me to dominate the market.

Here's one of my secrets for property evaluation: If you see properties with those 2020-era, $500 all-in-one arcade games, that's fine; for better marketability and guest utilization, however, invest in Arcade1Up games. Get Frogger, Pac-Man, NFL Blitz, and NBA Jam. You can get five machines for the price of one standard unit. While competitors might have a single game, you can line up four or five in a converted garage or bonus room, significantly enhancing marketability. Look for these opportunities during the Super Grading process.

Beyond the Super Property Grader, I examine bedroom count versus square footage. This becomes particularly important in states restricting Accessory Dwelling Unit (ADU) listings and additional nonconforming bedrooms. For example, in North Carolina, I found two excellent deals. The first was listed as a four-bedroom but included a guest house with a full kitchen, a family room, and two en suite bedrooms. North Carolina regulations prevented listing these additional spaces. Many investors lazily view this as just a four-bedroom property, but when I saw 5,800 square feet, I knew there had to be more potential.

You'll often encounter three-bedroom, two-bath properties around 2,300 square feet. Here's an insider tip: the average three-bedroom, two-bath home is typically 1,500 to 1,600 square feet. When you spot that extra square footage, investigate deeper if the property interests you. Consider the potential for adding a fourth bedroom. Contact your buyer's agent (not the listing agent) to conduct a thorough walk-through and identify hidden opportunities.

Look for unfinished basements, large bonus rooms suitable for bunk rooms, and three-car garages that could be partially converted into game rooms while maintaining storage space. Storage is crucial, especially in smaller properties with one to three bedrooms. If you're self-managing, you need space for linens, cleaning supplies, and amenity items, like coffee bar supplies. We prioritize properties with ample storage. We often install magnetic locks on cabinets, convert larger kitchen pantries into supply storage, and optimize bedroom closets with hotel-style hanging racks and credenzas with luggage racks.

The primary consideration when evaluating a property is its proximity to traffic drivers. As mentioned in chapter 6, I avoid investing in Smoky Mountain properties that are, at a minimum, twenty minutes from Dollywood because there are already five to seven thousand short-term rentals between my property and the attraction. This could lead to negative reviews, even if you manage to secure bookings. We must be transparent and focus on proximity-based investments.

LOCATION VS. PROXIMITY

A former mastermind member and friend bought a riverside property, and I purchased one in the same market a year later, about forty-five minutes apart. While we both have riverside locations—a significant traffic driver—the proximity differs dramatically. My property sits thirteen steps from the water's edge. I can grill on my Traeger while fly fishing from my deck. Their property, though well located with good views (8/10), sits twenty-five to thirty feet above the river with no direct access. They have a 2/10 proximity score because guests must drive two miles to a boat launch, while I rate 10/10 for both views and proximity.

This proximity factor is crucial across all markets. In Nashville, the bachelorette capital of the world, proximity to Lower Broadway's bars and honky-tonks drives value. When comparing two properties scoring 85 on the Super Property

Grader, the one two blocks or two miles closer to the action will generate higher rental income.

When looking at beach properties, I've mentioned several times that tier-two locations can be excellent investments, particularly with views and beach access. In markets like Gulf Shores, Alabama, or Myrtle Beach, or Hilton Head (both in South Carolina), streets typically run parallel to the beach. This is different from Panama City's perpendicular layout. If someone has to walk multiple blocks to access a public beach, this indicates poor proximity. Limited views between beachfront houses also impact value. These factors must be considered during property evaluation.

WHAT MAKES IT UNIQUE?

After completing the Super Property Grader, analyzing locations and proximity, and finding a unique property within your asset class, it's time to focus on property uniqueness. The best unique properties have distinctive external features, like superior views.

What is the difference, then, between amenities and features and a property's uniqueness? You'll probably get as many answers as there are properties out there! Amenities and features can certainly add to a property's appeal, but that's not the endgame to a property being unique. If you are on the hunt for a truly unique property, you're looking for long-term protection.

You can add unique amenities like pools, barrel saunas, and hot tubs, but these additions don't provide the long-term protection I'm talking about. Just a short time ago, for example, I was the only short-term rental in Whitefish, Montana, with a hot tub, barrel sauna, and geodome combination; this didn't prevent competitors from replicating these amenities six months later.

What they can't replicate is my property's proximity or views. Finding my Montana property took two years, six months, and five days of patience, multiple site visits, and evaluating about a hundred properties. I waited for perfect river views and access, then strategically positioned those expensive amenities. The barrel sauna's glass doors offer unobstructed views up the river to Stillwater Lake and, on clear days, to the Canadian Rockies. Similar positioning maximizes the hot tub and geodome experiences. The key isn't just adding amenities; certainly, those are important, but long-term market protection comes from natural features. Natural features can't be replicated. Focus on what nature provided first, *then* enhance it with interior improvements.

Consider why people choose your market. Families rarely select their vacation destination based on a specific property; the decision hierarchy is typically market first, activities second, and accommodation (hotel or short-term rental) third. Only exceptional properties, like Disney-themed accommodations, drive destination choices. That's why I prioritize exterior features before interior improvements. While anyone can add murals, update kitchen cabinets, install new Samsung appliances, or upgrade bedding and ceiling fans to compete at the top level, natural uniqueness provides a lasting advantage.

RUN THE PROFORMA

After completing this analysis and the Super Property Grader, the next step is running the Proforma. You can access my Proforma template and watch a free twenty-minute training session with Jon, the Bank Whisperer, from my Super Team. This tool helps estimate gross revenue performance. Combine this with data analysis from the Super Property Grader, STR Insights, and AirDNA to create financially driven insights from multiple data sets.

With your property's intangible ratings complete, take the estimated gross revenue from AirDNA and STR Insights.

I average both platforms' projections when building the Proforma. The Proforma helps mitigate risk by analyzing expenses, revenue, and amortization calculations for both twenty- and thirty-year loans. Most people default to the longest terms, but I prefer the shortest term I can afford within my budget.

Another common mistake: underestimating expenses by using random averages. Request actual utility bills, pool maintenance costs, water bills, and property taxes through your buyer's agent. Gather real data for everything, including cable and internet, not just the average costs of each. Consider market-specific expenses, too—beach properties need trash service, mountain properties require snowplowing. First-time buyers, especially those new to a market, must be particularly thorough.

I recommend using the "just in case you fuck up" (JICYFU) methodology, a concept I borrowed from my professional golf days. In golf, yardage books include contingency measurements for when you hit into trouble—similar planning applies to property investment. Add 10 percent to your calculated annual expenses. If expenses total $87,000, for example, you'll add $8,700 to that total. Then, on the revenue side, if AirDNA projects $100,000 and STR Insights suggests $110,000, average them to $105,000 and subtract 10 percent ($10,500). If the

Proforma still shows profitability with at least a 7 percent return, you have a 20 percent safety margin.

Proforma

Projected Revenue
$105,000
-10%
= $94,500

Projected Expenses
$87,000
+10%
= $95,700

JICYFU: 20% Delta

This approach is crucial for new investors without established benchmarks. Even with my experience from owning over seventy-seven short-term rentals and consistently performing 52 percent above the 90th percentile in most markets, I still implement the JICYFU delta. This buffer helped when

I discovered unexpected expenses, like snow-plowing in Banner Elk, North Carolina, or when insurance doubled after Hurricane Sally hit the Gulf Coast in 2020. These are the kinds of surprises I want to help you prepare for when underwriting properties.

CHAPTER 8

OFFER TO CLOSE AND INSTALL (PLUS A SECRET BONUS)

Once you've identified your potential property, you're entering the most critical phase that will determine success or failure in your short-term rental investment: the offer and the close. Let's focus on the key priorities as you prepare to make your offer, starting with your agent selection.

CHOOSING AN AGENT

Let me be clear: you need an agent.

Too many new investors try to skip this step—especially if they're buying a FSBO (for sale by owner) property—thinking they'll save a little money or have more negotiating power by handling the deal themselves.

That's a huge mistake.

You don't save money by going solo. In fact, it often ends up costing you more—through poor negotiation, missed details, or failure to leverage key strategies (like the one I'm about to share with you). The seller typically pays the buyer's agent commission anyway, so it costs you nothing to have professional representation.

But here's the catch: not just any agent will do.

Your agent will make or break your deal. Whether you're pursuing multifamily units, condos, or single-family homes, you need someone who:

- Owns or manages short-term rentals themselves
- Knows the local regulations inside and out
- Understands revenue potential by neighborhood or zip code
- Can negotiate like a commercial investor—not just a residential one

You should interview them—they shouldn't be interviewing you. And no, your cousin who just got their license last year and "loves real estate" is not the right fit.

CONTRACT TO CLOSE

Once you're under contract, you enter one of the most critical phases in the entire STR investing journey: the Contract-to-Close window. This is where speed, preparation, and precision start to pay off.

By now, you should have already vetted at least ten lenders:

- two local commercial banks
- two or three credit unions
- two or three national lenders

The goal? To know exactly which loan products you qualify for before you ever write an offer.

If you haven't already, download the DTI calculator and revisit the Debt-to-Income (DTI) training with Brenna Carles from The Mortgage Shop. For example, if you earn $100,000 annually, plan to put $100,000 down on a $350,000 property, and carry an $1,800/month mortgage, you may not qualify for a conventional loan—but a DSCR (Debt Service Coverage Ratio) product might be perfect for you.

And remember: some lenders will stall on out-of-state investments, even if you have a great relationship with them. That's why diversifying your lender list is critical.

But locking in financing isn't the finish line. It's just the start. The following is everything else you need to handle before the ink dries at closing.

SOURCING FURNITURE, DÉCOR, AND AMENITIES

During this phase, do not wait to begin sourcing. Even if your renovation budget is minimal—say $20,000—you still need to be sourcing everything now:

- Furniture, beds, linens, and décor
- Murals, paint colors, and light fixtures
- Coffee bars, amenities, and kitchen setups

You should have a complete install plan and sourcing spreadsheet ready before your clear-to-close.

My wife, Brea, our Inner Circle Design Coach, teaches

this exact process through our mastermind, including her full spreadsheet system and install timelines for zero-to-five property investors.

One of the biggest mistakes I see new investors make? Waiting until after closing to start planning. That delay can cost you thousands. You want to be fully staged and live within days—not months—of closing.

VENDOR RELATIONSHIPS

This is just as important as furniture. Vendor relationships are the backbone of a successful STR.

During the contract-to-close phase, start interviewing cleaners and handymen immediately. These are the people who will help you maintain five-star reviews—and if you wait until after closing to find them, you risk launch delays and poor guest experiences.

Here's what I recommend:

- Get two or three quotes from professional cleaning companies in the area
- Ask if they've worked with STRs before (this matters— STR cleanings are not typical residential cleanings)

- Find at least one general handyman who can handle small fixes quickly
- For remote markets, look into property managers or cohosts who can act as your boots on the ground

Bonus Tip: Ask your real estate agent and stager who they trust. Most of my best vendors have come from word-of-mouth referrals inside the local STR community.

Delivery and Receiving

This is often overlooked but can destroy your timeline.

Start coordinating delivery and receiving plans now. If the property doesn't have a garage, consider:

- Self-storage units (many accept deliveries)
- PODS placed on-site or at your cleaner's property
- FedEx or UPS stores
- Launched Host—Kim Fitzpatrick's company offers full-service receiving and installation within seven days (launchedhost.com)

Why does this matter? Let's say you buy a $500,000 property with $100,000 down and a $400,000 loan at 7 percent interest. Your monthly mortgage alone is ~$3,000. Add utilities and insurance, and you're at $3,500+ a month.

The average new investor takes three months to launch. That's over $10,000 lost to carrying costs.

On a property that grosses $100,000/year, that's 10 percent of your total annual revenue—gone.

My wife and I average eleven days from close to launch; whether it's a one-bedroom ski condo or a twelve-bedroom estate, our system is designed to hit the ground running.

Insurance

Another key item: don't assume standard homeowner's insurance will cut it.

STRs require specialized policies that account for:

- Guest liability
- Loss of income
- Amenity risks (pools, hot tubs, etc.)
- Location-specific threats like hurricanes, wildfires, or snow damage

Some cities also require minimum liability thresholds or proof of vacation rental coverage. Talk to an agent who knows short-term rentals in that specific market. Ask what additional policies are common or required. It's not just about protecting your asset—it's about staying compliant.

This contract-to-close window is where your entire Proforma either holds up—or falls apart. Delays here are expensive.

When you're locked, loaded, and ready to move, the moment your agent says, "We're clear to close," you protect your profit and accelerate your timeline.

Then you can breathe. Because now, we get to the fun part.

CHAPTER 9

SETTING UP YOUR LISTING AND MARKETING

After closing, you enter the exciting phase: setting up your Airbnb and Vrbo listings, creating a direct booking website, and marketing your property. This is my favorite part because it's the gateway to maximizing return on investment (ROI). Let's start with listings.

THE POWER OF PHOTOS

As your property setup nears completion, prioritize hiring the absolute best photographer you can afford. I personally use Andrew Keller from Chattanooga, Tennessee, who travels nationwide and delivers exceptional results. In Banner Elk, North Carolina, his photos helped increase revenue by 21 percent for my second-best-performing property—and this was already a well-photographed, well-staged property. I strongly believe that his next-level quality made the difference.

When to Budget for Photos

Plan for this expense early—ideally, during the contract-to-close window. As you're sourcing furniture and finalizing design details, reach out to photographers, get quotes, and reserve your shoot date. You want them lined up and ready to go the moment your property is fully staged, ideally within the first week after closing. Don't wait until after the setup is done—photographers book out quickly, and delays here mean lost income.

Secure photos of sunrises and sunsets, but ensure they showcase your property effectively. A skilled photographer captures views from inside the family room or kitchen looking out over mountain ranges, ski resorts, lakes, or beaches. While a budget photographer ($300–$700) might save money up front, they could cost you thousands in lost revenue over three years. Investing $2,500–$3,000 in premium photography typically returns your investment within 200 days.

It doesn't have to be Andrew, specifically, but examine the photo quality when completing your Super Property Grader. Aim for professional-grade imagery—no iPhone photos or budget photography. Your listing is your storefront, and photos are the first (and often only) impression.

Photo Order

Once you have your photos, photo order becomes crucial for listing setup. Marketing through photo order is critical. Whether it's Montana mountain views or tier-two Gulf Shores properties, strategic photo placement helps dominate the market. STR Insights data shows water should appear first for lake, stream, or beach properties. Show outdoor views first—people book your market for outdoor experiences, whether that means beach time, skiing, boating, hiking, ATVing, Nashville nightlife, or Scottsdale golf. Your property is secondary to the destination.

Showcase outdoor amenities in your first five photos: fire pits, pickleball courts, pools, hot tubs. Then transition to activities. For Scottsdale properties, highlight putting greens, pools, and observation decks with Pinnacle Mountain views. Feature outdoor lighting—string lights, outdoor fixtures, and LEDs make a significant impact. Show fire pits or pools at sunset. Then display local activities—golf courses, Pinnacle Peak hiking trails, Salt River tubing—before moving indoors.

Photo order becomes even more critical inside. Avoid random, disjointed sequences jumping from basement to bathroom to laundry room. Instead, imagine proudly showing your property to a loved one. Walk them through naturally: enter through the front door into the family room; showcase statement pieces like a striking green couch; display the staged dining table; move through the kitchen; "walk" them down hallways, into the master suite . . . with its spa-like bathroom featuring rolled towels. Show the master bed with its eleven pillows—two king-size soft, two king-size firm, plus decorative pillows—and that signature furry throw blanket. Include the bench, area rug, and an eye-catching mural.

These design elements create uniqueness and marketability. Maintain consistency as you move through the house. Don't jump from the front door to the basement, game room to the backyard hot tub, then back to the kitchen. Follow a natural tour path.

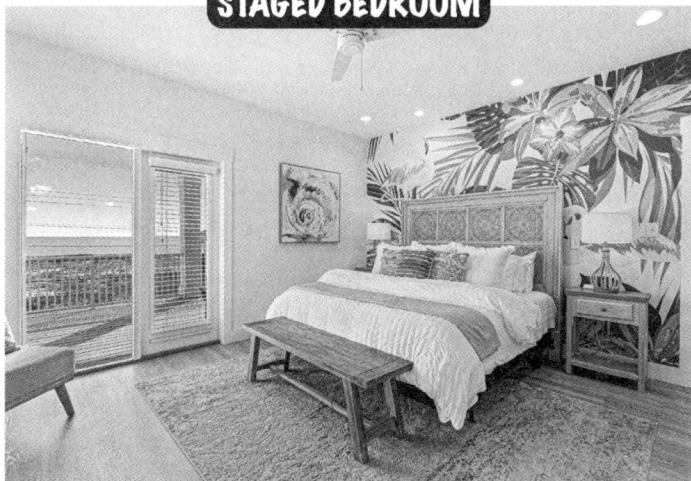
STAGED BEDROOM

Captions

Your photo captions should evoke emotion. Don't just list features like "king-size bed with TV and view." Instead, paint a scene: "After a long day at the beach, sink into your super-comfy king suite, enjoy an ice-cold bottled water (provided at every bedside), charge your devices with complimentary USB ports, and unwind with the 65-inch HD Smart TV. Refresh in the master en suite, featuring dual rain showerheads, soft Egyptian cotton towels, robes, and slippers."

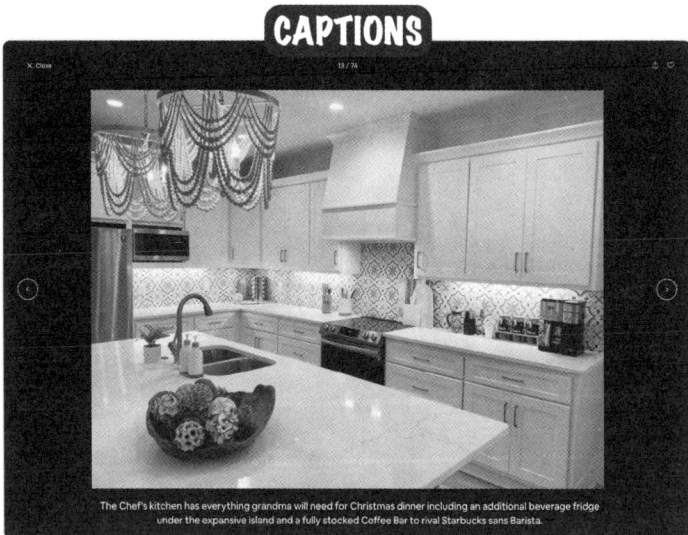

The Chef's kitchen has everything grandma will need for Christmas dinner including an additional beverage fridge under the expansive island and a fully stocked Coffee Bar to rival Starbucks sans Barista.

Sample Caption

The chef's kitchen has everything Grandma will need for Christmas dinner, including an additional beverage fridge underneath the expansive island and a fully stocked coffee bar to rival Starbucks, sans barista.

Show these amenities in sequence—bed, television, nightstand, followed by bathroom, rolled towels, and suite features. Transport viewers into experiencing your property. Focus on comfort and relaxation rather than just utility. Help them envision unwinding after an active day managing six kids from two families at the beach.

PRICING SOFTWARE

After your Airbnb and Vrbo listings are live, your next step is implementing pricing software. This is not optional if you want to outperform your market and avoid leaving money on the table.

When to account for the cost: I recommend including pricing software in your initial setup budget. Plan for this expense during the contract-to-close phase, just like you would for photography, furnishings, and design. Pricing software typically runs between $15-$40/month per property, depending on the platform and number of listings. If your first booking goes live without dynamic pricing in place, you're already behind.

I personally use PriceLabs, but there are a few solid alternatives:

- Wheelhouse
- Beyond Pricing
- Futurestay (best for beginners)

If you're just getting started and managing one to three properties, I highly recommend Futurestay—it's an all-in-one platform that includes:

- Built-in dynamic pricing
- Direct booking website
- Automated guest messaging
- Airbnb synchronization
- And more

You can check it out at futurestay.com/bill for a special discount I've arranged.

Pro tip: Futurestay works best for solo investors and small operators who want to keep things lean, simple, and centralized. It's great for properties in vacation-driven, highly seasonal markets where automation can reduce response times and maximize high-season rates.

For those planning to scale up to five to ten owned or cohosted properties, I also recommend OwnerRez (online at ownerreservations.com). I use both Futurestay and OwnerRez because they each shine in different areas:

- Futurestay is my go-to for properties where simplicity, quick setup, and done-for-you tools make the biggest impact—especially in markets where I want to be hands-off but still optimize my earnings.
- OwnerRez is ideal for more complex setups or multi-property portfolios, especially in heavily regulated or urban markets where you need granular control. Its integrations with accounting, insurance, and CRM tools make it a powerhouse for growth-minded hosts. One standout feature is its channel bridge tool, which syncs listings across all platforms while allowing for advanced pricing rules and adjustment strategies based on seasonality, occupancy, and lead time.

MARKETING AUTOMATION

Once your pricing strategy is in place, your marketing strategy needs to follow.

That's where MarketMySTR.com comes in. It's my go-to for automating:

- Email marketing to past guests
- Text message campaigns
- Direct booking website creation and hosting
- Weekly marketing tasks I used to spend 10–15 hours per week handling myself

Since I started using it, I've seen a 25 percent increase in repeat bookings and, more importantly, a massive reduction in manual work. This frees me up to focus on higher-level strategy and acquiring the next Super Property.

MARKETING ON FACEBOOK

Start with Feeder Markets

Before you can market your property effectively, you need to understand who you're marketing to. That starts by identifying your top feeder markets—the cities or regions where your guests are most likely to come from. These are the areas where you'll direct your ads, post in local Facebook groups, and eventually retarget for repeat bookings.

How do you figure out your feeder markets? There are a few simple ways:

1. Ask your property manager or local realtor. If they specialize in short-term rentals, they often already know where most guests are coming from.
2. Use your own data. If you've already had bookings, check Airbnb's "Where your guests are from" insights.
3. Check your competition. Scroll through reviews on other high-performing Airbnb or Vrbo listings in your market—reviewers' city and state often appear in their profiles.
4. Leverage STR Insights. It's a powerful tool that shows guest origin data for many markets.
5. Talk to local tourism boards or chambers of commerce. They often have visitor demographics you can use.

Once you've gathered this info, make a list of your top five feeder cities. For example, my Gulf Shores properties primarily attract guests from:

- Dallas
- St. Louis

- Indianapolis
- Chicago
- Nashville

This list is gold—it informs everything you do from a marketing standpoint.

Build a Facebook Presence

The easiest, lowest-cost way to start marketing is to create a Facebook page for your property. Don't overthink this. You don't need thousands of followers—the page's main purpose is to give you a home base for running Facebook ads.

My go-to strategy: the Dollar-a-Day Method. I spend just $1 per day, or $30/month, driving traffic to my:

- Airbnb listing
- Vrbo listing
- Direct booking site

That traffic improves visibility in search algorithms and helps convert browsers into bookings. With just a couple of hours of training, running these ads becomes a hands-off process.

Leverage Buy-Sell-Trade Groups

Once your page is live, it's time to get scrappy. Join 10–15 Buy-Sell-Trade or Local Events groups on Facebook in each of your top five feeder markets. These are free and full of potential guests.

Post weekly in a rotation, sharing:

- Seasonal promotions
- "Plan your getaway" inspiration
- Family-friendly or pet-friendly highlights
- Special event weekends or holidays

Personalize your replies using names. Even small things like "Hey Russell—yes, we're available that weekend!" or "Hi Lisa, here's a link to our dog-friendly listing" make a huge difference in conversion.

Stack Your Strategies

These three Facebook marketing pillars generate nearly 50 percent of my direct bookings:

1. Buy-Sell-Trade Group Posts
2. MarketMySTR Email + Text Automations
3. Dollar-a-Day Facebook Ads

Currently, I sit at 48 percent direct bookings, and these strategies are a huge reason I'm able to perform 52 percent above the 90th percentile in revenue for my markets.

Don't wait for traffic to find you on Airbnb and Vrbo—drive it yourself.

LISTING OPTIMIZATION

Listing optimization is crucial. Use Rankbreeze.com to track your Airbnb search rankings—because where your listing shows up directly impacts your visibility, pricing power, and ultimately, your bookings.

Your page position can affect your nightly rate by up to 30 percent. Showing up on page three of Airbnb search results versus the top five spots on page one is the difference between mediocre and high-performing cash flow.

When I say "optimize everything," here's what I mean:

- Photos: Use professional, high-quality images. Your lead photo (the first image people see) should be your most compelling outdoor view or standout feature.

- Headline: This is your listing's first impression—use clear, engaging language that highlights what makes your place unique.
- Description copy: Focus on clarity, benefits, and guest experience. Break it into short sections and use bullet points to highlight amenities.
- Host profile: People book from people. Add a friendly, trustworthy bio and upload a professional (or at least well-lit) profile photo.
- Neighborhood details: Highlight walkability, proximity to attractions, and anything that enhances the guest experience.
- Guidebooks: Add local recommendations using Airbnb's guidebook feature—this builds trust and gives guests more reasons to book.
- Check-in instructions: Clear, well-organized instructions reduce guest friction and improve your review scores.

Once everything is polished, update your listing twice a week, and track changes using Rankbreeze.

For example, try swapping out your lead photo or rewording the first paragraph of your description. Wait forty-eight hours to allow the Airbnb algorithm to react, then check your Rankbreeze dashboard. If your listing drops in rank (say from #3 to #6 on page one), revert the change. If it improves (e.g., from page three to two), log that update and keep going.

Pro Tip: Only make one change at a time. Otherwise, you won't know which edit caused the movement.

This kind of deliberate testing—what used to be called test marketing—applies across your business, from Facebook ads to email campaigns. It's how you go from average returns to top-tier performance.

Marketing and optimization are what separate good properties from Super Properties. While a great location and smart design set the foundation, it's these ongoing tweaks that help you dominate your market.

That said, marketing can become a serious time-suck. So next, let's explore smarter ways to make marketing work for you—without eating your entire week.

CHAPTER 10

TECHNOLOGY AND AUTOMATION

Short-term rentals differ significantly from traditional long-term rentals, starting with the need for consistent guests, cleaning and turnover responsibilities, and maintenance management. I typically send an average of twelve pre-canned and automated messages to guests, particularly in markets with longer lead times (the period between booking and stay). This includes six to seven pre-check-in messages.

Since this chapter focuses on technology, let's explore how to automate these processes efficiently, whether you're juggling a W-2 job or managing kids at home. We'll examine technology solutions for both small-scale (one to five properties) and larger operations (five or more properties).

PROPERTY MANAGEMENT SYSTEM

Let's start with Property Management Systems (PMS). If you own anywhere from one to five properties, I recommend Futurestay. You're already familiar with this company, as we discussed its pricing capabilities in chapter 9.

Futurestay founder Phil Kennard is an industry expert, and the platform offers direct development access through my Inner Circle. Their direct booking website conversion rates are outstanding, making it an ideal "easy button" for new hosts managing a small portfolio.

If you have or plan to build a larger portfolio of properties, I would strongly recommend OwnerRez, which in my opinion is the gold standard for enterprise property management systems. OwnerRez can handle the largest of portfolios with integrated messaging, a unified inbox, API integrations with QuickBooks and Facebook, synced calendars and much more to make your life as a large host easy.

REVENUE MANAGEMENT
AND DYNAMIC PRICING

You'll also recall PriceLabs from chapter 9, and it is essential for revenue management and dynamic pricing. Their market research reports are invaluable, and I find their platform more intuitive than Wheelhouse or Beyond Pricing. And yes, even if you're in the one-to-five properties category, this tool is absolutely worth it.

Why? Because you can't just "set it and forget it" if you want to outperform the market.

PriceLabs gives you two massive advantages:

- **Dynamic Pricing Engine**—Automatically adjusts nightly rates based on demand, seasonality, day of the week, local events, and historical trends.
- **Market Dashboards & Comp Set Reports**—Let you monitor local competition, understand occupancy rates, and adjust your pricing accordingly.

Even with just one property, these tools help you avoid leaving money on the table or pricing yourself out of bookings.

Beyond Pricing charges both a flat monthly fee and 1 percent of gross revenue, which adds up fast. PriceLabs, on the other hand, has a better pricing model and offers more powerful market insight tools, all within a cleaner, more intuitive interface.

Bottom line? If you want to maximize cash flow, stay competitive in your market, and avoid constant manual adjustments. PriceLabs isn't just a nice-to-have—it's essential.

MARKETING PLATFORM

Another name that should already be familiar to you, since I mentioned it in chapter 9: MarketMySTR. This platform serves as your comprehensive all-in-one marketing platform that is specific for short-term rental owners and cohosts. It enables automation of my 260-day rebooking funnel, text messages, and—if you're cohosting—includes CRM capabilities. The platform offers voice drops (direct-to-voicemail messaging) and numerous marketing features. While it might seem overwhelming, just focus on the four core features initially.

It's more cost-effective than combining separate services like Constant Contact, SimpleTexting, custom website development, and email automation tools. It may seem like a lot of front-loading, but once you've done the initial work, it just takes off and manages it for you. Over time, you can build out and add additional features to your marketing mix, but those four core features are robust enough to get your marketing moving seamlessly.

DIGITAL GUIDES

For digital guides, I prefer Touch Stay. I document everything from Schlage lock operation (automated smart locks that do a lot of back-end monitoring) to hot tub instructions.

Through Touch Stay, I can also include detailed photos of kitchen cabinet contents with annotated guides, showing locations of items like pizza cutters and wine glasses. Video content helps guests understand more complex amenities, like hot tubs or barrel saunas. The platform's intuitive interface allows easy integration of Google links for restaurant recommendations, hiking trails, and other local attractions. I share this guide two to three weeks before check-in, enabling guests to plan and pack accordingly. Think of this as the personal concierge you provide each guest.

SAFETY AND SECURITY

Since you can't be everywhere all at once, you need to have some safeguards in place to protect your property from vandalism, squatters, and thieves. Even the safest locations cannot be guaranteed to be 100 percent safe all the time—and why would you want to take that risk, given the time and resources you have spent?

For security, I use Ring cameras with battery power and solar panels, eliminating hardwiring needs. I standardize systems across all properties, owned or cohosted: Ring cameras, Schlage Encode locks, and ecobee thermostats. This consistency is nonnegotiable—I won't use different systems because managing multiple apps defeats the purpose of automation. This standardization helps me manage twenty-seven properties, and it probably costs me just three or four hours of my time each week (excluding time spent on pricing and marketing). For properties with pools, I recommend the Pentair app; it has automatic links that efficiently manage multiple pools through a single interface.

For larger portfolios (containing five or more properties), two major changes occur, while other systems remain constant.

First, OwnerRez becomes the preferred PMS, offering more robust enterprise features, enhanced reporting, and better API integration with QuickBooks, Vrbo, Facebook, and Google. Second, Breezeway becomes essential for streamlining operations and safety protocols. Justin Ford's safety course through Breezeway can even help secure insurance discounts.

Breezeway also offers cleaner scheduling integration. While I currently use ResortCleaning due to established processes, I'd recommend Breezeway for new operators seeking comprehensive handyman management and cleaner communication features.

BOOKING WEBSITES

Even if you're brand new to the short-term rental industry, you are likely already familiar with booking websites and how they work. When managing my own properties' bookings, I avoid expensive WordPress solutions requiring ongoing maintenance and hosting. Instead, I use sales pages designed for conversion by combining Futurestay and MarketMySTR. You can access my templates through MarketMySTR and integrate with Futurestay at futurestay.com/bill. This will provide you with a high-converting direct-booking system.

GUEST COMMUNICATION

Guest communication requires both automation and a personal touch. When someone books, I immediately record a personal welcome video: "*Hey Bob, thanks for booking [property name]. I wanted to put a face to the name. Please reach out if you need anything before check-in.*" This builds rapport and trust, particularly important given the 48-hour penalty-free cancellation window on Airbnb and Vrbo.

With my average booking lead time of 110 days (typical for vacation markets; urban properties average 10-20 days), message timing becomes crucial. Between booking and the check-in message (sent three days prior), I provide comprehensive local information—dolphin cruises, sunset tours, oyster bars for beach properties—referenced in the Touch Stay guide shared two weeks before arrival.

This communication strategy aims to build rapport while minimizing manual interaction. For common issues, like hot tub operation, create dedicated video guides rather than burying instructions in lengthy messages. On arrival day, send a focused message with the five most critical details: parking location, correct entrance, keypad operation tips (like using a phone flashlight at night), etc.

Keep messages focused and specific rather than

overwhelming guests with information. Create templates for common situations and maintain clear, bullet-pointed communications. This approach reduces guest queries while maintaining high service levels through automation.

Automation isn't just limited to guest communication. There are a few tools you can use that will actually do a better job than you will (yes, I said that!).

CHAPTER 11

PRICING OPTIMIZATION

New hosts often make a critical mistake with their first Airbnb: manual pricing. They start by setting uniform daily rates, then progress to basic weekend/weekday differentiation—perhaps $300 for weekends and $200 for Sunday through Thursday. This flat-pricing approach severely limits your revenue potential. The first step in optimizing your pricing is implementing a revenue management tool.

REVENUE MANAGEMENT TOOLS

While PriceLabs, Wheelhouse, and Beyond Pricing dominate the market, and all are certainly good tools, I personally recommend PriceLabs for its superior usability and marketing dashboard. The basic subscription costs about $18 monthly; it's worth it to level up and invest the extra ten bucks for the market dashboard, allowing you to track competitors from your Super Property Grader and monitor their pricing strategies.

Once you've set up a PriceLabs account, begin by establishing your low, medium, and high pricing tiers. Immediately after creating your listing, you'll want to identify premium dates—Christmas Day, New Year's Day, local fall break, local spring break, Memorial Day, Independence Day, and peak-season periods. You should already know what your peak season periods are, since you did your market research (review chapter 6 if you need a refresher). You will set rates for premium dates at least 30 percent higher than your average.

For instance, if your standard rate is $500, your premium pricing should start at a minimum of $650 per night. This strategy is critical because once someone books at a lower rate, platforms like Airbnb and Vrbo make it nearly impossible to cancel or raise the price without penalties.

Also, keep in mind that demand will shift—and your pricing needs to shift with it. There will be times when you should raise your rates due to increased demand, like upcoming events, festivals, or compression periods. Other times, you might need to lower your prices to stay competitive during shoulder seasons or unexpected market dips.

DYNAMIC PRICING

PriceLabs excels by generating dynamic pricing based on your parameters while factoring in market demand. When your area hosts major events, like a cheerleading competition with four thousand participants, the system adjusts rates based on market inventory. Understanding your average lead time—how far in advance guests typically book—becomes crucial for revenue management. For example, with a 100-day average lead time, you should price dates 250–365 days out significantly higher, especially during peak seasons (Memorial Day through Labor Day for beach properties; Christmas through mid-April for ski properties). Trust me, some people start looking as soon as they leave! You don't want your pricing to get stuck in the standard-rate gap when you could get your premium rate.

PRICING STRATEGY

Your Super Property Grader score also influences pricing strategy. When it comes to knowing when to adjust, timing is everything.

If your properties are scoring 91 when competitors average 70s–80s, these types of scenarios warrant aggressive pricing.

For lead times exceeding 200 days, increase your rates by 50–75 percent.

For properties scoring around 80, with several competitors in the 90s and others in the 70s–80s, you'll want to adjust to more moderate pricing. As you approach your average lead time (e.g., 100 days), implement the PriceLabs rule that will reduce prices 3–5 percent weekly, targeting optimal pricing by 100 days, pre-check-in.

Within 100 days, focus on competitive pricing and discount accordingly to secure bookings. I employ a "3-2-1 strategy," even in traditional markets like the Outer Banks, where my two properties near Duck, North Carolina, typically require Saturday-to-Saturday, seven-night minimums. It works like this: I allow three-night weekend stays, two-night weekday stays, and, crucially, one-night minimums within fourteen days of arrival. I guess maybe, for guests, this would be a case where if you snooze, you *don't* lose? As a property owner, however, I'd rather have a discounted booking than no booking at all. Let's examine my reasoning a bit closer.

While some might question offering one-night stays for large, six-bedroom beachfront properties commanding $4,000 nightly during summer, this strategy works effectively, particularly for Sunday through Wednesday bookings. Most guests traveling to distant locations with large families naturally book multiple nights, even when single nights are available. This flexibility helps fill "gap" nights—those single, vacant nights between bookings. For these gaps, approach departing guests about late checkout or extra nights first (since they're already there), or incoming guests about early check-in or additional nights. These up-sell and down-sell tactics optimize occupancy and boost revenue.

For those lacking time or interest in mastering revenue management, professional revenue managers typically achieve 30 percent revenue increases in comparison to skilled self-managers. While typical hosts need six to nine months to develop effective pricing skills, professional management can make a dramatic, positive impact on returns. In other words, what you pay in will likely pay out many times over. If this sounds like a plan, there are several good ones out there. I use Emil Sakhel at Pricing by Mira (pricingbymira.com). Emil's expertise transformed my Outer Banks properties from a projected $800,000–$825,000 annual gross revenue combined to tracking over $1 million for 2025.

Whew, we've almost made it to the end. Hopefully, you have a firm grasp on how to build your own portfolio of Super Properties. Want to know a little more? Turn the page.

CONCLUSION

THE ENTIRE COUNTRY IS YOUR OYSTER

Many new investors instinctively look in their backyard for their first property. But in writing this book, developing my coaching programs, and establishing the Build Short Term Rental Wealth community, I've aimed to equip you and other investors for successful self-managed remote hosting anywhere. Think of the entire country as your oyster.

As you now know, my own journey began with a property in Gulf Shores, Alabama, while living in Nashville, Tennessee—a seven-hour drive, or a flight plus driving time away. Were we nervous when taking over from the property manager who sold us the house? Perhaps slightly, but success in remote hosting primarily comes down to mindset.

My background actually gave me an advantage in remote hosting. Growing up without a father meant I never learned traditional home maintenance skills like changing tires, fixing leaky toilets, or repairing ceiling fans. This taught me early on to rely on professionals. Whether a property is next door or in Montana, I follow the same process: call a plumber for plumbing issues, contact HVAC specialists for climate control problems, or have cleaners address hot-tub concerns. Most issues receive attention within forty-five minutes to an hour, and my comprehensive Touch Stay guide provides video tutorials for amenity operation, from hot tubs to barrel saunas, arcade games, and Roku TVs.

My extensive messaging strategy—welcome videos, bullet-pointed communications, and targeted updates—serves a dual purpose. It enhances guest experience by anticipating and answering questions while minimizing direct communication needs. When issues arise, my reliable local teams handle them efficiently. The combination of technology, proactive communication, and Touch Stay guides makes remote hosting surprisingly manageable.

Instead of limiting myself to Nashville's market, I've diversified across beaches, lakes, mountains, and desert locations. Proper preparation eliminates the need for extensive weekly management time. The key is finding quality cleaners and handymen (or handywomen, like our cleaner/handywoman in North Carolina) through Facebook groups and community referrals. Our Build Short Term Rental Wealth group, with over 33,000 helpful hosts, provides valuable connections in almost every market. They want to help you succeed.

At this point, don't feel as though you have to have all of this committed to memory. Use the book as a reference when you need it. If I had to select the essential items I hope you've grasped, it would be these:

1. **You are investing in a property, not a market.**
   Don't chase social media hype or blindly follow trending markets. Focus on finding unique, high-potential properties—even in less obvious locations.

2. **Underwrite every deal with discipline.**
   Use the Proforma to run good, better, and best scenarios. Always invest based on the good—or maybe better—not the best.

3. **No stories.**
   Don't talk yourself into a bad investment by romanticizing a property. Stick to the data.

4. **Go where others aren't.**

   There's wealth to be made in secondary and tertiary markets—especially when you know how to identify compression events, amenities that outperform, and undervalued submarkets with upside.

5. **Operate with systems and tools.**

   Whether you're managing one property or twenty-seven, the systems in this book (Proforma, DTI Calculator, Super Property Grader, Touch Stay, MarketMySTR, Futurestay, and OwnerRez) make it scalable and sustainable.

6. **Build a portfolio that works for you, not one that owns you.**

   The 250 Plan isn't about stacking doors—it's about building net income with fewer, better-performing properties.

As of this writing, I successfully operate twenty-seven properties spanning from the Outer Banks to Glacier National Park, Gulf Shores, Banner Elk, and Arizona, all using the systems and technology outlined in this book.

When you leverage the provided resources—the Proforma,

Super Property Grader, the DTI calculator, and technology stack—you too can maximize your investment potential. Imagine the opportunities when you can use STR Insights to identify the most profitable gross ROI opportunities nationwide rather than limiting yourself to your local market.

This is the proven approach to building Super Portfolios.

CONNECT WITH ME

While our journey through this book may be wrapping up, your path to building a Super Portfolio is just getting started—and you don't have to do it alone.

I'm still in your corner.

Scan the QR code that follows to connect with me directly on Instagram, join our Build Short Term Rental Wealth Facebook group, and access more free tools and trainings.

Over the course of thirty-seven startups, one truth has stayed consistent: success is never a solo game. Surround yourself with people who are doing the work, ask better questions, and keep moving forward.

Can't wait to see what you build.

—Bill

ACKNOWLEDGMENTS

For Brea—thank you for being with me every step of the way and for pushing me to be a better husband, father, and provider. We have built many successful companies together, but nothing compares to the life we have built together with you as the leader.

For Oaklee and Gentry—you blow my mind every day, as you are so much smarter and better than I ever was at your age. I am completely in awe of what you two have accomplished and can't wait to see how you better the world as adults.

Love, Daddy

ABOUT THE AUTHOR

Bill Faeth is a serial entrepreneur, investor, speaker, and the founder of the #1 short-term rental brand (Build STR Wealth) in the industry, with a track record of building and scaling thirty-seven companies across multiple industries and generating more than $1 billion in lifetime sales. He is also the founder of the sold-out STR Wealth Conference, and his insights have been featured on Fox, Fox Business, NBC News, Merit Street, and other major media outlets. Beyond business, Bill is a dedicated family man who shares his success with his wife, Brea, and their two amazing daughters, Gentry and Oaklee.